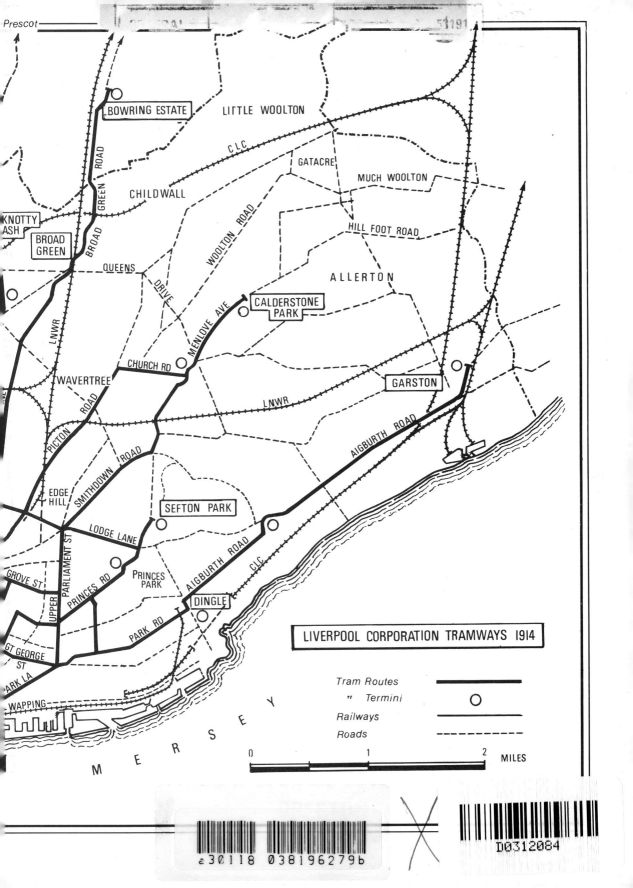

Prescot

BOWRING ESTATE

LITTLE WOOLTON

CLC

GATACRE

MUCH WOOLTON

CHILDWALL

BROAD GREEN ROAD

HILL FOOT ROAD

KNOTTY ASH

BROAD GREEN

WOOLTON ROAD

ALLERTON

QUEENS

DRIVE

MENLOVE AVE

CALDERSTONE PARK

LNWR

CHURCH RD

WAVERTREE

GARSTON

LNWR

ROAD

AIGBURTH ROAD

PICTON

SMITHDOWN ROAD

EDGE HILL

SEFTON PARK

LODGE LANE

PARLIAMENT ST

PRINCES RD

PRINCES PARK

AIGBURTH ROAD

CLC

GROVE ST

UPPER

GT GEORGE ST

PARK RD

DINGLE

ARK LA

WAPPING

M  E  R  S  E  Y

**LIVERPOOL CORPORATION TRAMWAYS 1914**

| | |
|---|---|
| Tram Routes | —————— |
| "  Termini | ◯ |
| Railways | ———— |
| Roads | — — — — |

0          1          2    MILES

# Roads, Rails & Ferries of
# LIVERPOOL
## 1900~1950

## J. Joyce

LONDON
IAN ALLAN LTD

# Bibliography

# Contents

**Books**

Anderson, R. C.; *A History of Crosville Motor Services*; David & Charles, 1981.

Box, Charles E.; *The Liverpool Overhead Railway 1893-1956*; Railway World, 1959.

Dibdin, H. G.; *Liverpool Tramway Album*; Author, 1972.

*The First Sixty Years*; Liverpool Corporation Passenger Transport Department, 1957.

Forbes, N. N., Felton, B. J., Rush, R. W.; *The Electric Lines of the Lancashire & Yorkshire Railway*; Electric Railway Society, 1976.

Holt, Geoffrey O.; *A Regional History of the Railways of Great Britain; Volume 10, The North West*; David & Charles, 1978.

Horne, J. B., Maund, T. B.; *Liverpool Transport*; Volume 1, 1830-1900; Volume 2, 1900-1930; Light Rail Transit Association/Transport Publishing Company, 1975/1982.

Jones, D. C.; *Survey of Merseyside*; Liverpool, 1934.

Lyons, David C.; *The Leeds & Liverpool Canal*; Hendon Publishing Company, 1977.

Martin, T. J.; *Liverpool Corportion Tramways 1937-1957*; Merseyside Tramway Preservation Society, 1972.

Maund, T. B.; *Local Transport in Birkenhead and District*; Omnibus Society, 1959.

*Southport Corporation Transport Department Centenary*; Southport Corporation, 1967.

*The Story of Merseyrail*; Merseyside PTE and British Rail, 1978.

Walker, Brian, Hinchcliffe, Ann; *In Our Liverpool Home*; Blackstaff Press, 1978

**Periodicals**

*Buses; Flight; Meccano Magazine; Modern Tramway; Modern Transport; Omnibus Magazine; The Railway Magazine; Railway World; The Shipbuilder; Tramway & Railway World* (later *Transport World*); *Tramway Review*.

Previous page: A summer day in Lord Street, Liverpool, in 1908; a continuous parade of tramcars, already with covered top decks to provide increased all-weather capacity, offers frequent service and low fares. 'Cheaper to ride than walk' was the aim of municipal policy. *H. G. Dibdin*

First published 1983

ISBN 0 7110 1306 3

Published by Ian Allan Ltd, Shepperton, Surrey; and printed by Ian Allan Printing Ltd at their works at Coombelands in Runnymede, England

# Introduction

If one element had to be identified as the basic influence on Merseyside's transport history it could well be the fact of isolation, paradoxical though this may seem in the case of a major seaport. Cut off on one side by the Mersey and on the other by a tract of wasteland, Liverpool's progress as a port depended on improved communications by road, canal and railway. At the same time, this heritage of isolation engendered a unique quality, not only in the city itself but in the transport network within Liverpool and its environs, and this individuality persisted at least until the formation of today's Passenger Transport Executive. It was reflected in the many disparate components in the transport pattern: railways, tramways, buses and ferries, owned and operated by municipalities and companies large and small, all with their distinctive character and often with conflicting interests. All had to be welded into one integrated whole, a process which offers a case study in transport evolution within the regional context.

Over the years the importance of the regional framework grew in significance, notably with the rise of the motor bus and the private car. No single community could be considered on its own; faster and more flexible travel modes enabled the built-up area to extend into a widespread Liverpool suburbia, along the Mersey estuary and up the coast, inland to coalesce with the Manchester conurbation, and across the width of the Wirral peninsula. The broader scale of operations demanded a broader view of both transport and planning; municipal boundaries had to be transcended and parochialism replaced by coordination.

Problems there were in plenty, and we can view these more sympathetically in that we have not solved all of them ourselves. Congestion and the place of the motor car, peak-hour traffic and the profitability of marginal services, investment in new facilities, coordination of operations, the relation between transport and planning — all these questions have long been centres of contention, and there is a certain fascination in looking back to see how our predecessors coped, perhaps over-optimistically believing that the definitive answers were imminent.

And what were the effects of transport developments on the lives of the people of Merseyside? Apart from the crucial links forged with other parts of the country by the improvement in roads and the growth of the railways, the provision of cheap and convenient local transit facilities not only revolutionised urban life, but also stimulated a redistribution of population away from the old overcrowded districts near the riverside to an extensive hinterland of new dormitory suburbs. Over the course of time, too, some of the modes earned a place in popular affection; the Overhead Railway, the trams and the ferries became established institutions which were as symbolic of the city as the Liver Bird itself. But change was inevitable as conditions imposed a standardisation over a wider area under the control of one centralised authority.

This book aims to survey a few of these themes: to observe the evolution of an integrated transport network within one region, its nature, its effects and its problems. Contemporary quotations and illustrations have been drawn upon freely, not only to remind us what the city and its suburbs looked like during the first half of this century, but also to reveal our predecessors' opinions and actions as they shaped the transport system we were to inherit. I can claim no originality in this book; it is not a formal comprehensive history — others more knowledgeable and competent than myself are undertaking that task — but I hope it may afford some interest to those who might wish to turn back for a moment from today's scene to recall yesterday's transport on Merseyside.

### Acknowledgments
My principal debt is to the printed word in both books and periodicals; the bibliography lists sources for those who might wish to verify (or dispute) my conclusions or to look further into any particular aspect of our subject. I owe a special debt to John Prigmore and the Librarian of the Lyon Playfair Library of Imperial College for granting me access to the resources of the Library. I am also grateful to Geoffrey Sandford especially for information on the Mersey ferries. No less am I indebted to the photographers who have searched their collections to find photographs to meet my requirements and have made prints available for the purposes of this book; particular thanks are due to Roy Brook, C. Carter, H. G. Dibdin, N. N. Forbes, and the late W. B. Stocks, as well as to the Ian Allan Library.

*J. Joyce*

# 1 Transport for a City

*During the last 60 years Liverpool has not only increased its population fivefold, but has itself been improved perhaps more than any town in England. It now has as handsome streets, as substantial dwellings, and as sumptuous public buildings as any city in the Kingdom.*
Morton's Railway Guide, 1879.

The historic overland approach to Liverpool lay through the forests of the Wirral peninsula and across the wide River Mersey by means of the Monks' Ferry. Daniel Defoe came this way in 1720 when he was carried ashore on the shoulders of a burly Liverpudlian wading kneedeep from the boat. He discovered a flourishing seaport which was 'one of the wonders of Britain', and concluded that 'there is no town in England that can equal Liverpool for the fineness of the streets'.

Liverpool's early eminence as a port depended on trade with Ireland, but its massive expansion to make it the nation's dominant shipping centre resulted from the Industrial Revolution, when England became 'the workshop of the world'. Cut off on one side by the river and on the other by a marshy wasteland or 'moss', Liverpool demanded improved communications in order to fulfil its new role. Until the middle of the 18th century roads were so bad that travellers were obliged to ride horseback to Warrington to catch the 'flying machine on steel springs' which made its way to London in three days. Before the end of the century a coach was running from Liverpool to London in 48 hours, while by the late 1830s this time had been halved by the best coaches such as *The Umpire* and *The Express*. By then too the railway age was well under way, following the opening of the Liverpool and Manchester Railway in 1830.

Water transport had also been improved; from the end of the 17th century, work on extending navigation on the Mersey was put in hand, while the Leeds and Liverpool canal — a waterway more than 120 miles long and taking 40 years to complete — linked Liverpool with the Lancashire coalfields and the industries of Yorkshire, bringing trade to and from the port. Along the waterfront a line of docks was constructed, eventually extending a distance of some six miles from Dingle to Seaforth.

Liverpool's population was increasing rapidly during the 19th century; from only 80,000 in 1800 it more than quadrupled to some 375,000 by 1851 and then almost doubled again during the next 50 years to reach more than 700,000 by 1901. Prosperous merchants made their homes on the higher ground in districts such as Mossley Hill, Sefton Park and Aigburth, or by the sea at Waterloo and Crosby, commuting daily by coach or omnibus. The working classes were concentrated in a semi-circle of a mile or so radius from the city centre, along Scotland Road to Bootle or to Edge Hill and Everton, often in conditions of extreme overcrowding. In the absence of cheap mass transit facilities most workers had to live near their place of employment — in Liverpool's case, the docks and warehouses that lined the riverfront. Across the water, Birkenhead (which developed its own industries, notably shipbuilding) and Wallasey were growing as dormitory areas for the better-off, who used the frequent services of steam ferries, and later the Mersey Railway under the river.

Within Liverpool itself, improvements were not only providing the populace with amenities such as the parks around the edge of the city, but were also facilitating the operation of local transport. The tradition of street widening had obviously started by the latter part of the 19th century, judging by a contemporary description of 1880: 'The best streets are no longer narrow, their direction is calculated to utilise them to the full as main arteries of traffic, and no enterprise or expense has been spared to raise upon their sides magnificent shops, warehouses and other buildings worthy of a city which takes so foremost a place in trade.'

Along these streets the tramcar and the omnibus were initiating a new era of local movement. A 'railway omnibus' had run on the Liverpool dock railways in 1859, and in 1860 George Francis Train had inaugurated in Birkenhead the first 'street railway' to be constructed in Britain. Train was also responsible for Liverpool's first tramway, in 1861, but this proved to be short-lived. However, under the auspices of the Liverpool Tramways Company, first formed in 1865, routes were constructed to Dingle in 1869, to Walton in 1870 and to Aigburth Vale in 1871. The company merged in 1876 with the Liverpool Omnibus Company to form the Liverpool United Tramways and Omnibus Company which by the 1890s was operating more than 200 tramcars and over 100 buses.

Significant to the future development of the local

6

Top left: One of the smartest coaches, the Liverpool *Umpire* made the journey to London in 24 hours in the 1830s.

Centre left: The railway's triumphal entry to Liverpool: the famous Moorish Arch of the Liverpool & Manchester Railway at Edge Hill.

Below: The progress of rail transport: a full-scale replica of Stephenson's *Rocket* of 1829 for the Liverpool & Manchester Railway contrasts with 20th century motive power, LNWR 4-4-0 No 2155 *W. C. Brocklehurst* of the 'George the Fifth' class introduced in 1910. Built at Crewe in 1911, the replica *Rocket* later starred in the railway centenary celebrations in Liverpool in 1930. *Ian Allan Library*

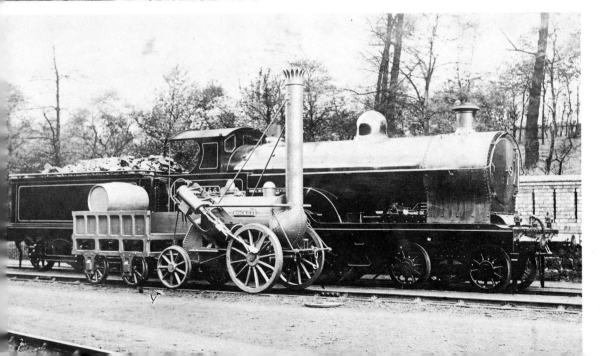

Left: Liverpool towards the end of the 19th century: the concentration of the city into a comparatively small densely-packed area within the ring of hills is obvious. Walton and Toxteth Park are still rural (as witness 'Lodge Farm' and 'Brook Farm') though the railways are encouraging suburban living. The line of docks is already extensive and the dock railway is prominent; the Overhead Railway has not yet been built. On the Birkenhead side are Seacombe Ferry, Woodside Ferry, Monks Ferry (by Woodside station), Birkenhead Ferry and Tranmere Ferry; the Mersey Railway is not yet shown.

Below left: 'Liverpool has as fine public buildings as any city . . .' St George's Hall in the days when the tramcars were still horse-drawn. *R. Brook*

Above: A reminder of horse-car days: centre-groove rail used by the Liverpool United Tramways & Omnibus Company before the lines were relaid by the Corporation for electrification after 1897. This section survived amid the setts in Great Charlotte Street to be photographed in the 1930s, and was still there in the 1980s. *W. B. Stocks*

Bottom: The electric tramway era gets under way; Derby Square, Liverpool, at the turn of the century presents quite a cosmopolitan air with two 'pagoda-roof' German 4-wheelers and an American bogie car, representative of the city's earliest electric car fleet. *N. N. Forbes*

282.

New Brighton. At the same time, the big main-line companies stimulated traffic to and from their own local stations; abundant services and cheap season ticket rates had already helped to transform districts such as Childwall, West Derby and Gateacre into favourite places of residence for Liverpool businessmen. The continued initiative evinced by the railways ensured that their services remained an integral sector of the region's transport network even

Below: *Daffodil*, one of the best-known of the Mersey ferries, carries a capacity load on a breezy day with flag flying proudly. Later named *Royal Daffodil*, she was taken out of commission in 1933 after 27 years of active life, to be replaced by *Royal Daffodil II*. The Wallasey and Birkenhead ferry services were notable examples of municipal enterprise. *N. N. Forbes*

transport system was the process of municipalisation. Liverpool already boasted a long tradition of municipal enterprise; it had built docks, markets, warehouses and bath-houses, and it had been the first city outside London to undertake the building of council dwellings. Electricity supply was taken over by the Corporation in 1896, so the extension of municipal operation to the city's transport seemed a natural evolution; accordingly the Liverpool United Tramways and Omnibus Company was acquired by the Corporation in 1897. This move was soon followed by the electrification of the tramways, with the first electric cars starting to run in the succeeding year, and soon spreading so rapidly that the last of the horse-drawn vehicles were superseded in 1902.

The impact of the electric tramcar may be gathered from a contemporary description dating from 1903, by A. H. Beavan in his *Tube, Train, Tram and Car*: 'The new cars are remarkably fine and comfortable, and include the Continental single deck with a side entrance, and the double deck with doors at the end and with three large well-curtained plate glass windows on each side. No one can grumble at the fares charged, which are at the rate of one penny per stage of two miles. That these tramways are a great boon is shown by the enormous numbers of passengers — near 100 million — carried last year.'

The next few years witnessed further rapid development, and the position of the tramways in their heyday can be judged from a glance at the three neighbouring Merseyside systems in 1911. The giant was of course the network operated by Liverpool Corporation, which in that year served a population of more than 800,000 people. It owned a fleet of about 570 cars working over 116 miles of track and running at an average speed of $7\frac{1}{2}$mph, carrying 130 million passengers who were able to ride $2\frac{1}{2}$ miles for 1d. Traffic receipts amounted to over £600,000, while the gross operating profit was more than £200,000. Capital expenditure on the system amounted to close on £2 million. Within the city boundaries you could make a continuous journey by car from Aigburth to Fazakerley or Aintree, a distance of more than eight miles, or travel a further eight miles around the 'outer circle' route. With only one change of car you could ride the 12 miles from Pier Head to St Helens.

In comparison both the Birkenhead and Wallasey undertakings were on a much smaller scale, though nevertheless substantial. Birkenhead Corporation served a population of some 130,000 with about 60 cars, which carried just over $12\frac{1}{2}$ million passengers on the 24 miles of track along the docks as well as to suburban homes. Traffic receipts amounted to about £57,000, with a gross operating profit of some £22,000, while capital expenditure had reached more

than £360,000. The average speed attained by the cars was less than 7mph, while a penny fare took you less than $1\frac{1}{2}$ miles. Wallasey Corporation, marginally the smallest of the triumvirate, served a population of some 78,000 people, with 55 cars averaging 7mph on 20 miles of track and carrying 10 million passengers in the year, many of them excursionists and holiday-makers enjoying the sea breezes of New Brighton. For a penny you could ride more than $1\frac{3}{4}$ miles. Gross profit was nearly £17,000, with traffic receipts of £50,000, while capital expenditure amounted to over £200,000.

Added together, the three undertakings amounted to quite a formidable business enterprise, representing a capital of more than £$2\frac{1}{2}$ million and with a turnover approaching £$\frac{3}{4}$ million a year. Not only was this a substantial vested interest which might well be slow to react to changing circumstances, but it stood firmly backed by the municipal coffers fed by the local ratepayers, and by the municipal authorities armed with powers designed to ensure that outsiders did not encroach upon their respective territories. Little wonder that the emerging bus operators, flourishing in the 1920s under the impetus of rising demand and unregulated conditions but often with limited financial resources, were to look enviously at the rich lands within the jealously-guarded municipal boundaries.

The extent to which the tramcar was essentially a short-distance means of transport was revealed by the fact that in one year (1905) almost 90% of the total number of passengers on the Liverpool system travelled at the 1d fare. About 9% were conveyed at the 2d fare. In that the 1d fare was valid for a distance of about $2\frac{1}{2}$ miles, its preponderance is not surprising in view of the still limited size of the city and its suburbs and consequently the limited length of the routes. Nevertheless, while the penny fare continued to be the mainstay of the undertaking, the expansion of suburbs and routes over the years gave scope for longer-distance travel; the corresponding figures for 1914 were already suggesting this tendency, in that the proportion of 1d fares had decreased slightly to under 88% of the total while the 2d fares had increased to 11%. Suburban termini were as far-flung as Fazakerley, West Derby, Edge Lane, Calderstones and Garston, while the new suburban role of the tramways was symbolised by the construction of the Broad Green and Bowring Park line in 1914-15.

Meanwhile, the railways also played their part in the area's travel pattern, contributing not only to intra-urban traffic but also to the suburban ebb and flow. Some lines were essentially local in character, like the Liverpool Overhead which gave access to the many docks as well as to the suburbs of Seaforth and Dingle, or the Wirral Railway which connected with the under-river Mersey Railway to serve Wallasey and

# 2 On the Waterfront

## Transport in Dockland

*The most striking view of Liverpool is that presented from the deck of one or other of the splendid fleet of steamships that ply upon the waters of the Mersey. Besides the host of river steamers that run up and down or across the stream, larger vessels carry on daily communication with Dublin, Belfast, Glasgow, the Isle of Man, Cork and other parts of the United Kingdom; while others, more spacious and more powerful still, are engaged in the trade with North and South America, Spain, Portugal and the Mediterranean.*
Morton's Railway Guide, 1879

A new era opened for Merseyside after the creation under an Act of 1857 of the Mersey Docks and Harbour Board to take control of the docks in both Liverpool and Birkenhead. There followed decades of expansion when Liverpool was the major port for industrial England, sending out manufactured goods to the world and taking in the raw materials and foodstuffs to feed the factories and factory workers. Famous shipping lines established themselves in Liverpool: names such as Bibby, Blue Funnel and Booth, White Star and Cunard, Canadian Pacific, Anchor Line and Harrison Line were famed on the seas of the world.

Dock expansion only drew to a close during the trade and shipping depression of the 1920s and 1930s; the Gladstone dock, the last major extension of the system, was in hand before World War 1 but was delayed by wartime conditions and was eventually completed in 1927 in very different circumstances from those in which it had been conceived. Nevertheless, Liverpool retained its position as the United Kingdom's largest exporting port, while in imports it was second only to London. Even in a depressed year such as 1931-32 it dealt with upward of 1,900 ships. More than six miles of docks and basins had a water area totalling 475 acres, while the total length of quays was 29 miles; to these figures, Birkenhead added 170 acres and 9 miles.

For the passenger, the focal point of the docks — and indeed of Liverpool itself — was the Prince's Landing Stage, a half-mile long floating platform constantly busy with hurrying crowds and vessels of many kinds. The northern half of the stage was used by steamers to Ireland and the Isle of Man as well as serving the giant trans-Atlantic liners. The southern half was reserved for the ferries, which maintained an intensive service with the several landings on the Cheshire side of the river: Seacombe, New Brighton, Egremont, Woodside, Rock Ferry and New Ferry. Gangways led from the landing stage to Riverside station for trans-Atlantic passengers, and to the Pier Head where streams of tramcars and omnibuses served all parts of the city.

Typical activity at the landing stage as it was at the turn of the century is recalled in this contemporary description:
'The landing stage is used by the steam ferry boats across the Mersey, and by the steamers which go coastwise and to the Isle of Man. It is from this stage that passengers embark to go on board the ocean-going steamships which cross the Atlantic and which are now so numerous that one belonging to one or other of the lines — Cunard, Inman, White Star and so forth — leaves Liverpool on every day of the week. A small steam tender lies alongside the stage to receive its living freight: Americans returning from a trip to Europe and the old country, men of business bound for Boston and New York, perhaps some star of the London stage about to make a professional tour in the States. Here land also the rough tars, Jack ashore after a long voyage, with his bag and baggage and his pockets well lined, to be wasted ere long in riotous living.'

Liverpool owed its earlier growth as a port largely to the Irish traffic, which long remained an important part of its trade. 'Liverpool every summer suffers an invasion of the sons of Erin', wrote a contemporary describing the annual influx of Irish workers who came to help with the harvest in England. They were able to voyage over on the steamer from Dublin for only 5s (25p) though apparently, when their pockets were full after the season's labours, they were charged a good deal more for the return journey.

At the start of the 20th century, representative of the Anglo-Irish link was the night steamer of the City of Dublin Steam Packet Company, whose vessels were 'fast and powerful, and fitted with every modern convenience, such as electric light, thus offering the traveller a comfortable and unbroken night's rest'. Departure from Dublin was at 8pm and the crossing

Top: Municipal pride: the crew of Wallasey Council Tramways No 12 pose for the photographer before taking their car on to the road. One of the original batch of 1902, No 12 at first had an open upper deck but was soon fitted with a covered top. *H. G. Dibdin*

New Brighton. At the same time, the big main-line companies stimulated traffic to and from their own local stations; abundant services and cheap season ticket rates had already helped to transform districts such as Childwall, West Derby and Gateacre into favourite places of residence for Liverpool businessmen. The continued initiative evinced by the railways ensured that their services remained an integral sector of the region's transport network even into the age of the motor vehicle.

And, perhaps the most characteristic part of the transport scene, the ferries shuttled tirelessly across the Mersey, carrying more than 20 million passengers a year on the Seacombe boats and over 10 million on Woodside. 'Next best thing to an ocean cruise' and, more prosaically, a notable example of municipal enterprise, how could one imagine the waterfront without *Royal Iris* or *Royal Daffodil*?

Below: *Daffodil*, one of the best-known of the Mersey ferries, carries a capacity load on a breezy day with flag flying proudly. Later named *Royal Daffodil*, she was taken out of commission in 1933 after 27 years of active life, to be replaced by *Royal Daffodil II*. The Wallasey and Birkenhead ferry services were notable examples of municipal enterprise. *N. N. Forbes*

# 2 On the Waterfront

## Transport in Dockland

*The most striking view of Liverpool is that presented from the deck of one or other of the splendid fleet of steamships that ply upon the waters of the Mersey. Besides the host of river steamers that run up and down or across the stream, larger vessels carry on daily communication with Dublin, Belfast, Glasgow, the Isle of Man, Cork and other parts of the United Kingdom; while others, more spacious and more powerful still, are engaged in the trade with North and South America, Spain, Portugal and the Mediterranean.*
Morton's Railway Guide, 1879

A new era opened for Merseyside after the creation under an Act of 1857 of the Mersey Docks and Harbour Board to take control of the docks in both Liverpool and Birkenhead. There followed decades of expansion when Liverpool was the major port for industrial England, sending out manufactured goods to the world and taking in the raw materials and foodstuffs to feed the factories and factory workers. Famous shipping lines established themselves in Liverpool: names such as Bibby, Blue Funnel and Booth, White Star and Cunard, Canadian Pacific, Anchor Line and Harrison Line were famed on the seas of the world.

Dock expansion only drew to a close during the trade and shipping depression of the 1920s and 1930s; the Gladstone dock, the last major extension of the system, was in hand before World War 1 but was delayed by wartime conditions and was eventually completed in 1927 in very different circumstances from those in which it had been conceived. Nevertheless, Liverpool retained its position as the United Kingdom's largest exporting port, while in imports it was second only to London. Even in a depressed year such as 1931-32 it dealt with upward of 1,900 ships. More than six miles of docks and basins had a water area totalling 475 acres, while the total length of quays was 29 miles; to these figures, Birkenhead added 170 acres and 9 miles.

For the passenger, the focal point of the docks — and indeed of Liverpool itself — was the Prince's Landing Stage, a half-mile long floating platform constantly busy with hurrying crowds and vessels of many kinds. The northern half of the stage was used by steamers to Ireland and the Isle of Man as well as serving the giant trans-Atlantic liners. The southern half was reserved for the ferries, which maintained an intensive service with the several landings on the Cheshire side of the river: Seacombe, New Brighton, Egremont, Woodside, Rock Ferry and New Ferry. Gangways led from the landing stage to Riverside station for trans-Atlantic passengers, and to the Pier Head where streams of tramcars and omnibuses served all parts of the city.

Typical activity at the landing stage as it was at the turn of the century is recalled in this contemporary description:
'The landing stage is used by the steam ferry boats across the Mersey, and by the steamers which go coastwise and to the Isle of Man. It is from this stage that passengers embark to go on board the ocean-going steamships which cross the Atlantic and which are now so numerous that one belonging to one or other of the lines — Cunard, Inman, White Star and so forth — leaves Liverpool on every day of the week. A small steam tender lies alongside the stage to receive its living freight: Americans returning from a trip to Europe and the old country, men of business bound for Boston and New York, perhaps some star of the London stage about to make a professional tour in the States. Here land also the rough tars, Jack ashore after a long voyage, with his bag and baggage and his pockets well lined, to be wasted ere long in riotous living.'

Liverpool owed its earlier growth as a port largely to the Irish traffic, which long remained an important part of its trade. 'Liverpool every summer suffers an invasion of the sons of Erin', wrote a contemporary describing the annual influx of Irish workers who came to help with the harvest in England. They were able to voyage over on the steamer from Dublin for only 5s (25p) though apparently, when their pockets were full after the season's labours, they were charged a good deal more for the return journey.

At the start of the 20th century, representative of the Anglo-Irish link was the night steamer of the City of Dublin Steam Packet Company, whose vessels were 'fast and powerful, and fitted with every modern convenience, such as electric light, thus offering the traveller a comfortable and unbroken night's rest'. Departure from Dublin was at 8pm and the crossing

Above: The Liverpool waterfront at the end of the 19th century; sailing ships and paddle steamers cross and recross the Mersey. In the background can be seen the landing stage for the ferries.

Below: A cold crossing! Passengers brave the elements as Wallasey ferry *Crocus*, festooned with icicles, ploughs its way across an ice-strewn Mersey in the winter of 1898. *Edward R. Dibdin*

H.M.S. MAURETANIA.

Left: Liverpool as a transatlantic port: the Cunard White Star liner *Scythia* is manoeuvred to the landing stage at Easter 1937. Dating from 1920, the *Scythia* was an oil-fired turbine-driven 20,000-tonner. Rationalisation had led to the merger of the two famous shipping lines Cunard and White Star in 1934.   *W. B. Stocks*

Above: Cigarette cards enlarged youthful local knowledge: one of a series on 'Merchant Ships of the World', this one featured the most celebrated ship to grace the Mersey, the Cunard liner *Mauretania* of 1907, 'the fastest ocean-going liner afloat' and holder of the Blue Riband of the Atlantic for 22 years. Withdrawn in 1935, she was succeeded by a new *Mauretania* launched in 1938.

Below: Silhouetted against the setting sun spectators young and old find the activity at the landing stage a never-ending fascination. One ferry takes on its passengers while another is in mid-stream in this photograph from 1933.   *W. B. Stocks*

took about eight hours. On arrival at the landing stage at Liverpool in the early morning, the traveller who wanted to continue his journey found the Lancashire & Yorkshire Railway (L&YR) omnibus waiting to convey him and his baggage free of charge to Exchange station to catch a train to Manchester or York. For those who were not in a hurry, or who desired to 'prolong their rest' on the steamer, 'the omnibus is again in attendance at the stage at 7.30am to convey passengers to the station, where they can breakfast at the company's hotel (one of the most comfortable in Great Britain)'.

Departure of the Dublin and Belfast night steamers could be a lively occasion, since both were due to leave the landing stage at around the same time (commonly 10.15). As this hour approached, the stream of vehicles bringing passengers and baggage increased, mingling with the confusion of those who tried to board the wrong vessel. Busy periods such as the Whitsun or August holidays saw the connecting trains run in duplicate to deal with the crowds, with resultant delays beyond the scheduled time as the last of the passengers made their way from station to landing stage. More confusion could reign if for some reason a change had to be made to the routine; a Cunard or White Star ship, normally berthed at Gladstone dock, might be found alongside the landing stage due for sailing at 10 o'clock, and passengers for Dublin would be told that their own steamer was at the Gladstone dock, three miles away.

There was an element of rivalry to see which could be away first: the green-funnelled Dublin steamer or the red-funnelled Belfast. One departure would hasten the other, and the two would hurry away down the Mersey almost side by side, through the narrow channel past the lights of the seafront, nearly to the Crosby lightship, before they diverged to take up their respective courses. Passengers could watch the lights of the rival ship gradually disappear into the distance as both steamers raced full speed ahead to make up lost time and achieve a punctual arrival at their destination.

From the Collingwood dock, the L&YR's own steamers for a time operated a twice-weekly service to Drogheda. Star of the line was the twin-screw *Colleen Bawn*, introduced in 1903 when it was enthusiastically described as 'this admirably equipped steamer, lighted throughout with electricity, and with dining saloons, ladies' cabins and state rooms replete with every modern comfort'. Her sister ship the *Mellifont* spent some time at Goole, where most of the L&YR's shipping interest was concentrated, but returned to the Drogheda service in 1912. Under an Act of 1902 the L&YR had acquired the Drogheda Steam Packet Company and its four steamers, which were withdrawn between then and 1912 in favour of the two new

ships. In its turn the LMS, as successor to the L&YR, gave up the service in 1928 to the British and Irish Steam Packet Company, and both the *Colleen Bawn* and the *Mellifont* were transferred to Holyhead.

On the Isle of Man service, the steamers of the Isle of Man Steam Packet Company were renowned as among the largest on the short-sea routes. The company, which is happily still in existence, can trace its origins back to 1830 when the paddle steamer *Mona's Isle I* was able to make the Liverpool-Douglas crossing in eight hours. By contrast *Mona's Isle III*, built in 1882 and in service up to World War 1, could reach a speed of 18kts and complete the crossing in about $3\frac{1}{2}$ hours; capable of accommodating more than 1,500 passengers with a crew of 56, she was the company's largest and most luxurious vessel. She was eclipsed in 1908 by the new *Ben-my-Chree*, which could take some 2,500 passengers and attain about 25kts, so bringing the crossing down to little more than three hours. The Isle of Man became one of the favourite holiday resorts for the people of Lancashire, and in a typical year before World War 1 the Steam Packet Company's fleet of 15 steamers on its various services carried a total of more than a million passengers.

Another popular holiday voyage from the Mersey was to the North Wales coast, to which services were provided by the steamers of the Liverpool and North Wales Steamship Company. A reporter of 1909 was among the holidaymakers arriving at Central station, from where 'we are hurried away by bus to the landing stage where the paddle steamer *La Marguerite* is embarking her passengers'. The voyage begun, 'the murkiness of Liverpool, with its warehouses and docks, is in marked contrast to the wild and mountainous country which lies before us as our steamer approaches Llandudno'. *La Marguerite* became something of an institution during more than 30 years of service, eventually being replaced in 1926 by the new twin-screw turbine steamer *St Tudno*.

For a great port Liverpool seemed strangely deficient in its facilities for the convenient transfer of passengers between rail and steamer. On arrival at Central, Lime Street or Exchange, passengers bound for the steamer had to make their way through the streets of the city to reach the landing stage, and fleets of wagonettes, omnibuses and taxis (and later Corporation motor buses) were provided for this purpose. A familiar sight was the latecoming vehicle, perhaps delayed by traffic or a mishap over luggage, hurrying on to the pier as the vessel was about to cast off. The problem was never satisfactorily solved; the busy landing stage remained without rail service to or from the main stations, and the great trek of luggage-encumbered passengers continued to symbolise one of the hurdles to easy travel.

Right: Liverpool for the Isle of Man: the Cheshire Lines railway advertise their services in connection with the Isle of Man Steam Packet Company in this Edwardian poster.
'Passengers travel by Express Trains to Liverpool Central. Passengers and their Luggage are conveyed between the Central Station and the Landing Stage Free of Charge and thence forward by the Splendid Saloon Steamers of the Isle of Man Steam Packet Company.'

Below: The Mersey scene in the 1920s: tramcars negotiate the turning circles at the Pier Head while shipping throngs the river; smoke from the ferries rises above the gangways, while a large steamer stands further along the landing stage. *R. Brook*

Eventually a station was in fact built adjacent to the landing stage. This was Riverside, opened in 1895 and conveniently placed for passengers to make a simple transfer from train to ship by crossing the platform and ascending the gangway. But in practice Riverside offered only a very selective contribution towards resolving the problem. Spurred by the competition with Southampton for the American traffic, Riverside was constructed by the Liverpool steamship companies and was normally used only by special LNWR boat trains, but such were the physical and operational limitations that the railway company was happy if its use was restricted to two trains a week.

To reach Riverside the boat train from London, acclaimed as 'one of the very "crackest" of crack trains in the country', had to diverge from the main line at Edge Hill, squeeze through narrow goods tunnels, cross dock tracks where shunting locomotives manoeuvred the port's freight, and end up trundling through the streets preceded by a man with a red flag. Such a tortuous course was imposed by the topography of the city and the layout of the docks, but it was not conducive to the working of a high-speed intensive train service. The CLC had also tried running an experimental train from its Brunswick Docks station, but had found it so impracticable that the idea was not pursued.

The LNWR's 'American Specials', which were run twice a week into Riverside to connect with the New York ships of the White Star and Cunard companies, were the pride of the line. Made up of the latest 12-wheel coaches, a train typically carried up to 100 first-class passengers, 20 second class and 20 third class, their needs ministered to by a staff comprising two guards and two train attendants, plus two waiters and two cooks in the kitchen. The exclusive character of the train was emphasised by the fact that only first class passengers were permitted to enter the dining saloons — after all, anyone who could afford to go to America ought to be able to afford to travel first class; the lower classes could be supplied with dinner baskets if they wanted them.

'American Specials' were hurried from London to Liverpool in four hours, but half an hour of this was occupied in negotiating the section from Edge Hill to Riverside. At Edge Hill, the express locomotive was detached and two tank locomotives were attached. For many years these comprised a pair of 0-6-0 saddle tanks dating from 1875 and 1876 respectively, and bearing the names *Liverpool* and *Euston*. Fitted with square-section tanks and condensing apparatus, they became a distinctive sight, the more longlived of the two surviving until 1939. Their place was taken by 0-6-2T 'coal tanks', another type long familiar on Merseyside; it was not until the final years that the big

express engines were permitted to run right through to Riverside.

The arrival of the 'Special' is well recalled in a contemporary description from the turn of the century:
'The luggage was handled out of the vans by LNW men, and then taken off in trolleys by the steamship companies' porters, of whom sometimes a hundred are employed for the purpose on heavy days. Alongside the landing stage lay the fine steamer *Germanic* belonging to the White Star line, with her head pointed down the river, and a crowd of steerage passengers on her decks watching the arrival of the "saloons". Everything was done so swiftly, methodically and quietly that it might have been simply an ordinary cross-channel boat instead of an Atlantic "greyhound". Half-an-hour is allowed for the transference, and long before this time had elapsed the very last passenger and his portmanteau were on board, and the landing platform cast off, the lookout posted on the crow's nest on the foremast, the Captain and Queenstown pilot on the bridge, and exactly on the stroke of five the good ship *Germanic* was gliding from the landing stage.'

After World War 2 the glory of the trans-Atlantic liner traffic had faded in the new era of mass air travel. In its final days Liverpool's Riverside station saw no more than one or two trains a week, until it was eventually closed in 1971. As a reminder of a past age when travel conditions were vastly different from those we know today, it would be hard to better a description given by the LNWR's General Manager, Frederick Harrison, in one of *The Railway Magazine's* 'Illustrated Interviews' in 1897:
'We have undoubtedly laid ourselves out for the American traffic, and it is an open secret that we have been successful in securing the cream of it. Every time one of the Cunard or White Star steamers sails from Liverpool we run a special timed to connect with it at the Riverside station in Liverpool ... The trains are thoroughly up to date, with corridors throughout and containing dining saloons in which lunch or dinner is served ... We sometimes have to run two specials for one steamer ...

'I think a journey at the present time from London to New York exemplifies to a very high degree the extent to which luxury and convenience have been carried in modern travel. A family staying in London and wishing to get to America have really nothing to do but pack their trunks and send for one of the Company's omnibuses, and from the moment they step into it they are relieved of all trouble and anxiety, either as to themselves or their luggage. Arrived at Euston they find the "Special" waiting, and in the time they have lunched or dined, they find themselves at the Riverside station, where they simply have to alight and walk a

Above: Liverpool as a link in the 'All Red' route to the East: 'Euston & Japan in $22\frac{1}{2}$ days' by means of the 'All British Route via Liverpool, Montreal and Vancouver'. The LNWR and the Canadian Pacific Railway, one of the major shipping lines operating into Liverpool, made this Edwardian round-the-world journey look easy.

Below: LNWR 0-6-0 saddle tank *Euston*, with its companion *Liverpool*, for many years hauled boat trains on the tortuous line between Edge Hill and Riverside. Dating from 1876 and 1875 respectively and fitted with square section tanks, both locomotives survived until the late 1930s when their role was taken over by 0-6-2 'coal tanks'. *Ian Allan Library*

few yards across the landing stage to the steamer. There is not so much worry and fatigue now in going from London to New York as there used to be going from London to Manchester.'

The aura of opulence surrounding the passenger traffic of the great liners does not obscure the importance of the freight upon which the livelihood of the port basically depended. And serving the miles of docks were the railways which carried the millions of tons of freight every year.

For its part in the port's trade, the L&YR maintained six major depots, as well as a number of smaller stations, along six miles of Liverpool's dock area. They ranged from the North Mersey and Alexandra Dock station in the north to the South Docks depot, traffic being collected and distributed by way of the marshalling yards at Aintree and Fazakerley Junction. While all depots handled the traffic of their respective docks, with cotton naturally featuring prominently, some developed their own specialities.

The North Mersey depot, for example, was adjacent to the massive grain elevators of the Liverpool Grain Storage and Transit Company, while it also later served the Gladstone dock where the largest Atlantic liners were berthed. North Docks depot specialised in cattle, with extensive accommodation for the large number of animals brought over from Ireland; Saturday night and Sunday morning witnessed the departure of the 'cattle specials' bound for the Manchester market. Coal was also handled, brought in by the high level coal railway of the Mersey Docks and Harbour Board; this elevated line at one point forced the Overhead Railway to come down to earth in order to get under its viaduct. Coal figured largely also at Canada Dock, where the tips despatched some two million tons a year for exports and ships bunkers. To cater for the needs of the coal trade, for which the L&YR was the leading rail carrier into Liverpool, special sidings were laid down at Sandhills and Fazakerley to accommodate more than 3,000 wagons from the trains of 60 to 90 wagons coming over the Pennines from the Yorkshire collieries.

The LNWR also had its own outlets in Liverpool's docks. From Edge Hill, the Waterloo line plunged into its tunnel to reach the Waterloo goods depot, while another line ran to Wapping, and the Bootle branch gave access to both Alexandra and Canada docks. Connections were made with the Harbour Board's tracks, and for long the LNWR employed a series of 0-4-2 tanks to operate its own traffic within the docks area.

Special interest of the LNWR naturally focused on its own docks at Garston. Located a few miles up the estuary, Garston was outside the control of the Mersey Docks and Harbour Board, thus allowing its owners a free hand in determining its charges. Its main trade was with the nearby industries in St Helens, Widnes and Warrington, taking coal out and bringing minerals and chemicals in. During its palmy days previous to World War 1, more than 4,000 vessels a year used the docks, and 18 locomotives were kept busy on the dock railways shunting about a million wagons a year. The LNWR had acquired Garston docks under an Act of 1864, taking over from the St Helens Railway & Canal Company and subseqently greatly extending the installations.

A speciality at Garston was the traffic in bananas. With the Fyffes Line vessels coming in once or twice a week, more than six million bunches of bananas could be landed in the course of a year. Elevators and conveyors were installed for the process of unloading, and as many as 30 special trains would depart with the cargo from one ship. In the course of a year a total of more than 1,600 trains would distribute the fruit to markets in London, the Midlands and Northern England, and Scotland.

Hub of the LNWR's Liverpool goods traffic was the great marshalling yard at Edge Hill, where trains to and from the various docks were assembled or broken up. A novel feature was the use of gravity for shunting the wagons; this was probably the first major adoption of this method of working, which was introduced when the yard was laid out between 1875 and 1882. Later widely employed on British railways, the gravity yard reduced locomotive power and speeded operations, as wagons were left to run down the gradient into their respective sidings, where they were brought to a halt by mechanical retarders — though horses continued to have a useful role to play in rescuing wagons which were inadvertently switched into the wrong sidings.

In its heyday the Edge Hill yard found employment for about a hundred men as foremen and shunters. The great expanse of tracks was usually quiet by day, but after nightfall it came to life as trains converged upon it from all directions to be marshalled and despatched; in the course of one night some 50 to 60 trains departed for their various destinations throughout the LNWR's network.

On the other side of the Mersey, Birkenhead docks penetrated more than two miles inland from the river, so that the unsuspecting visitor might suddenly encounter a ship apparently stranded high and dry in open country. The first Birkenhead docks dated from 1847, and early rivalry with Liverpool prompted the establishment of the Mersey Docks and Harbour Board as the overall authority for both sides of the river. Development then went ahead steadily, with the various docks — Alfred, Victoria, Wallasey, Egerton and Morpeth — providing facilities for such noted lines as the Holt 'Blue Funnel', the Clan and the City,

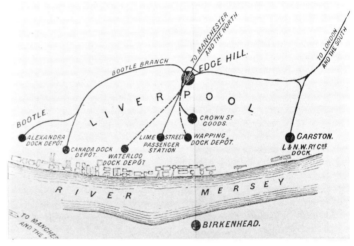

Top right: Liverpool docks at the turn of the century: a barge negotiates the dock entrance, while horse-drawn wagons plod across the bridge and in the background the Overhead Railway thunders past on its lofty viaduct.

Centre right: LNWR freight facilities in Liverpool's dockland, as depicted in Sir George Findlay's *Working and Management of an English Railway*, 1894.

Below: At the height of rail activity at the docks, the Mersey Docks & Harbour Board operated a fleet of more than 30 locomotives. Typical of the Board's fleet was No 21, an 0-6-0ST of Avonside design.
*W. B. Stocks*

trading with Africa, India and the Far East.

Cattle formed an important part of Birkenhead's import trade, with vast numbers landed at Wallasey and Woodside. Consequently 'Meat Specials' departed daily for all parts of England, with the LNWR, for example, running its expresses of meat vans to Manchester and Birmingham. Among exports, locomotives and rolling stock were often to be seen, bound for the overseas railways in which British capital had been invested: perhaps to South American lines to haul those very cattle which were shipped back to Birkenhead.

In addition to the main line companies, the Mersey Docks and Harbour Board also worked its own railway system, including the six-mile trunk line along the length of the Liverpool docks, together with the many branches and sidings connecting the principal docks themselves. Typical motive power for many years was the 0-6-0 saddle tank, and examples of these built in the first two decades of the century long formed the mainstay of the Board's stock of more than 30 locomotives.

# Liverpool Overhead

*Unique in that it traverses a great city and runs above ground for its entire length is the Liverpool Overhead Railway... It was the first electric railway of commercial importance in the United Kingdom.*
Railway Wonders of the World, 1935

An American from New York arriving in the Mersey for the first time was likely to be struck by a feeling of nostalgia as he neared the Liverpool waterfront; not only were ferry boats bustling across the river, but prominent on the skyline was an elevated railway. The Liverpool Overhead Railway (LOR) was the British equivalent of the American 'elevated' which served cities such as New York or Chicago; but the British had not only purloined the idea, they had stolen a march on the Americans by being the first to build an electrically operated 'El'. The LOR was not only the first of its kind in Britain (and was destined to remain unique) but also the first to adopt electric traction.

'Take the train to view the liners!' proclaimed the posters of the LOR, which was not slow to exploit the tourist potential of its six-mile grandstand fringing the string of docks. You could get round-trip tickets, with cut rates for parties, while the big shipping lines sponsored special excursions to enable sightseers (and, it was no doubt hoped, likely customers) to glimpse its ocean giants at rest. Not that this was the prime purpose of the Overhead; its real object was the more mundane one of conveying dock workers, shipping clerks, seamen and all who had business in the port, from one to another of the city's numerous docks.

The origin of the railway went back at least to the 1860s when some speedier means of transport was sought than the omnibuses that mingled with the shunting locomotives and goods wagons traversing the congested dockside thoroughfare. The solution was a railway carried on a viaduct above the roadway, and the first section of the Liverpool Overhead Railway — from Herculaneum Dock to Alexandra — was officially opened by ex-Prime Minister Lord Salisbury on 4 February 1893, though the public had to wait until 6 March before they were admitted. The northward extension to Seaforth Sands was opened on 30 April 1894 and the southward extension to Dingle on 21 December 1896. This latter section belied the railway's name by disappearing underground into a tunnel to reach its terminus.

For a description of the trains in their original form we may turn to the contemporary account by D. K. Clark in his *Tramways: Their Construction and Working:*
'One train consists of two carriages, each 45ft long and 8½ft wide, on two bogies 32ft apart from centrepin to centre-pin, with 2ft 9in wheels, 7ft wheelbase and pressed steel frames. The carriages are all exactly alike and contain accommodation for 16 first class and 41 second class passengers in each carriage, with three side doors and a passage from end to end. The first class passengers are at one end of the carriage, and the driver's box with switches etc is at the other. When the two carriages are coupled together to form a train, the driver's boxes are at the extreme ends and two first-class compartments consequently together in the middle of the train. A small door through the contiguous ends of the carriages enables the guard or attendant to pass from end to end of the train.

'The motors, one at each end of the train, are controlled from either end; the driver, of course, always travelling at the front end of the train and changing ends upon arrival at the terminus, carrying with him a key without which the motors cannot be operated.'

Clark would have felt at home here for most of the long life of the railway, for the trains changed remarkably little in appearance over the years, although the two-car formation was strengthened to three to meet traffic needs; towards the end, too, some of the trains were drastically rebuilt in smart modernised form, but generally the line seemed to be little affected by the passing of time.

As to what the traveller saw from his elevated vantage point in the heyday of the port, a patriotic geography lesson has been left for us by Beavan in his *Tube, Train, Tram and Car* of 1903:

'From the Overhead Railway a splendid view is obtained of the busiest locality perhaps in the Empire.

Top right: A continuous procession of carts and wagons thronged Victorian Liverpool's dock road; the Overhead Railway was to be the only answer to the need for rapid communication.

Centre right: The Liverpool Overhead as it might have been: the steam- worked New York 'Elevated' provided the inspiration for Liverpool's line which became the first to be operated by electricity.

Below: An Edwardian poster advertises the Liverpool Overhead Railway's speedy service not only to the docks but to sands, parks and suburbs. Special rates were offered to 'large parties of Excursionists'.

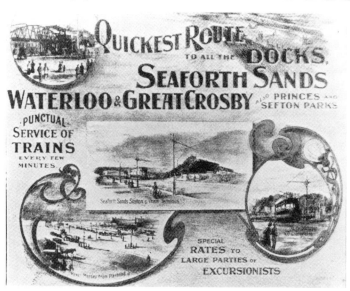

Top right: One of the lifting bridges on the LOR, installed to enable high loads to pass through to reach the docks.

Bottom right: A section of the LOR structure being erected by means of travelling cranes, a scene that could almost have inspired one of Liverpool's most renowned products, Meccano!

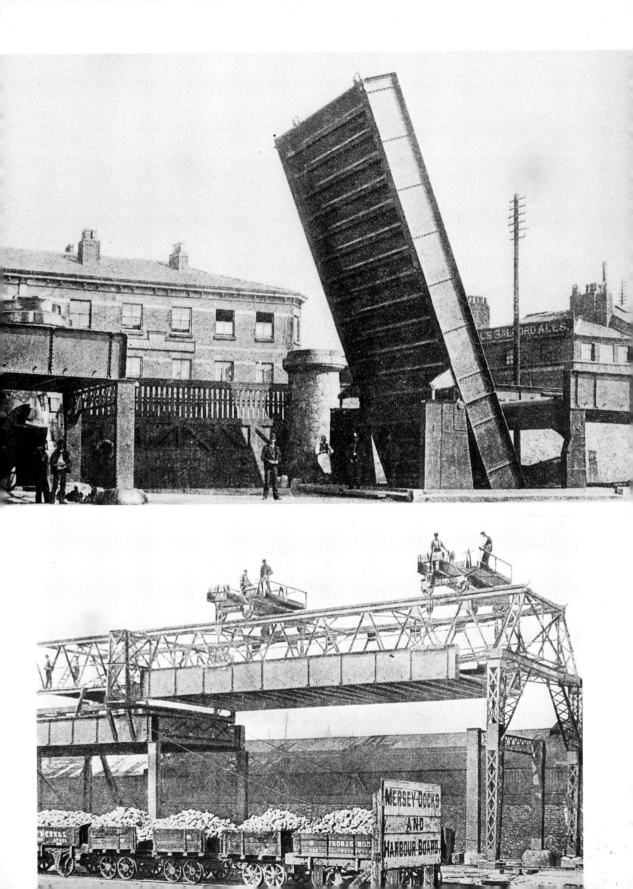

Above: The Liverpool Overhead Railway in operation; train No 17 negotiates the crossover at Canada Dock on Sunday when engineering work necessitated single-line working. *N. N. Forbes*

Below: For 60 years the viaduct of the Overhead Railway formed a background to the docks; the legend painted on the bridge proclaims 'Electric Railway. Trains Every Five Minutes'.

Below are the railway trucks packed close with imported merchandise of all kinds: cotton from America and the East; grain from the ends of the earth; beef, bacon, cheese, butter, flour and fruit from the New World; wool and tallow from Australia and Argentina. Wagons and carts filled with Manchester goods, hardware, machinery, chemicals, and every imaginable kind of manufactured goods, are alongside the big liners that come into port, discharge their cargoes, load up and are out in the Mersey and off to sea again in a few days. Truly Liverpool is a wonderful place . . . '

And wonderful it was too for the LOR while trade was thus flourishing in the port. But inevitably as a consequence of its specialised traffic, when trade fell off and fewer ships were loading and unloading in the docks, so the Overhead felt the chill winds; fewer people had business with ships and cargoes, so fewer people needed to travel on the railway.

Another baleful influence on the Overhead was the advent of the electric tramways. The first of the Corporation's new electric car routes as early as 1898 ran between the city and Dingle, the very terminus of the LOR. Although the journey took longer, fares were lower and there was the added convenience of a car at the street corner instead of a walk to the station and a climb on the stairs to the platform. Moreover the tram took you through the heart of the city instead of past a line of docks. The trams continued their advance northward so that before 1900 was out they had penetrated to the other extremity of the Overhead at Seaforth, so that the railway's whole length was under attack.

In an attempt to regain its deserting passengers the LOR tried the effect of speed. Trains were remotored to permit an acceleration of the schedule: the time for the journey was cut from more than 30 minutes to little over 20 minutes, thus raising the average speed from something over 12mph to nearly 19mph, a remarkable increase of nearly 50%. This brought something of the desired result; but it also brought less desirable side-effects in higher current consumption and greater wear and tear on track and rolling stock. The high-speed trains of the LOR therefore proved to be a short-lived phenomenon, and instead economy measures were adopted, such as the closure of some stations after the evening peak.

Trade fluctuations and the competition of other modes of transport were reflected in the railway's traffic figures. The 10 million passengers carried in 1900 were down to nine million by 1907, abstraction by the tramways being only partly compensated by the fast trains, while in that year a trade decline set in and the figure had dropped to eight million by 1909. World War 1 and the short postwar boom saw traffic rise to its all-time peak of 17 million passengers in 1919, but trade depression soon engulfed the docks and a low point of only about 5½ million passengers was reached in 1933. Again war brought a boom between 1939 and 1945 when the port was bustling with wartime activity, and the passenger figure increased to nearly 14 million in the busiest year. But a fall set in after the war; the 12 million of 1946 declined to fewer than nine million by the time the line closed in 1956, by which time bus competition had had its effects, as well as the long-term changes in the docks.

The need for costly renewal of the structure sealed the fate of the Overhead. Plans to save this Merseyside landmark included an idea for a Corporation takeover, but the trends were not favourable to any worthwhile future. The nature of the city was changing; the greatest days of the docks were passing, and population and industry were moving out of the central districts, while road transport had proved itself more flexible than the railway in that the bus could provide a network of direct services to all parts of the city and its suburbs.

The extensions to Dingle and Seaforth had been made to widen the scope of the railway; in addition to serving the docks themselves, it could also tap densely-populated residential districts and bring them into direct communication with docks and city. Writing about the Dingle extension, *The Railway Magazine* in 1898 pointed to the success of this new section, 'chiefly on account of the fact that the station is situate in the centre of a district thickly populated by working people who are thus enabled to reach the business parts of the town in a few minutes'. The role of the LOR was neatly summarised:

'. . . in facilitating communication between the residential districts at the south end of the town and the docks and business parts, in bringing the inhabitants of these districts within half an hour's run of Seaforth Sands, and in placing the splendid parks, which were hitherto but little known to any but their immediate residents, within the reach of the population at the north end of Liverpool, Bootle and Waterloo, and also within the reach of hundreds of thousands who cross the Mersey by the Mersey Railway or by the numerous ferries.'

Ironically, in the same year that these words were printed, the first of the city's electric tramways were inaugurated, to provide a serious competitor for the LOR's role.

Links with the L&YR — to Seaforth and the South-port line as well as annual jaunts to Aintree — further widened the scope of the LOR. But this was not intended to be all; *The Railway Magazine* in 1903 reminded its readers that 'when the Liverpool Overhead Railway was constructed the opinion was sometimes expressed that it was merely the thin end of the wedge for the creation of a belt railway'. The LOR formed the only connecting link between the railways north and south of Liverpool, and consequently there were 'enormous possibilities'.

The 'belt line' became a perennial element in plans to improve Liverpool's railway network; it was still being longingly looked at in some quarters as late as the 1960s. Basically the 'belt' involved an alliance between the LOR and the Cheshire Lines. Powers obtained in 1903 provided for a connection from the LOR at Herculaneum to St Michaels on the CLC's line from Central, while further powers in 1904 allowed for a connection at the north end of the LOR from Seaforth to the CLC at Sefton. With these two links, the 'belt' could have been completed, with the LOR forming one side and the CLC line between Gateacre and Sefton the other, thus giving a circular route connecting the Liverpool waterfront with the growing suburbs along the eastern edge of the city. The CLC's services by the end of the 19th century had already helped to develop suburbs such as Otterspool, Aigburth, Grassington and Garston, while on the other side of the 'belt' Childwall and Knotty Ash had already become 'favourite residences of Liverpool merchants', while Gateacre 'with its beautiful scenery' had been brought within 15 minutes of the centre of Liverpool. A less ambitious connection, consisting of no more than a half-mile spur at Aintree, was proposed later, but nothing materialised.

The obvious objection to the 'belt' was implicit in the name; while it may have served those who wanted to make a circular tour of the city, most people naturally wanted to go in or out of Liverpool in more or less a straight line, and for this purpose the railway would have been at a severe disadvantage. The distance from West Derby to Pier Head, for example, would have been 12 miles by 'belt' while the distance by road was only about four miles. Moreover, the more populous areas of the 'belt' were within the ambit of the Corporation's tramways, while the less populous parts were not yet likely to justify a frequent electric train service.

# Freight by Tram

*There is a scheme on foot in Liverpool for utilising the tramway lines in that city and the adjacent towns for goods traffic.*
The Engineer, 1903

Towards the end of 1902 representatives of Liverpool's Tramways Committee 'waited upon' the Mersey Docks & Harbour Board to submit a scheme for carrying freight over the city's tramways from the docks to the inland Lancashire towns. The deputation, it is reported, 'were met most cordially', and it was agreed that further details should be examined. The idea that the new electric tramways might play a part in the transport of merchandise seemed to offer considerable attractions at the time. In 1903 the South Lancashire Tramways Company envisaged that goods would be carried on its proposed 75 miles of routes from the Liverpool docks to the mills and factories of the hinterland. It proposed to run cars at night for this purpose, conveying freight direct from ships at Liverpool to depots and warehouses along the routes as far as Manchester and the surrounding towns. Special sidings at factories and collieries would enable the cars to deliver their loads, and a large number of manufacturers and colliery proprietors were reported to have agreed to the construction of such sidings into their premises to connect with the tramways. Daytime traffic would also be run, using special trailers for freight loads. It was believed that, because of the reduction on handling charges, such a method of operation would reduce the cost of transport by as much as 50% as well as proving just as rapid as delivery by railway.

The area served by the company's proposed network included the major industrial towns of the region, engaged not only in the cotton trade but also in manufacturing and coalmining, while the population numbered some $3\frac{1}{2}$ million. The scheme was taken sufficiently seriously for the formation in 1903 of the Lancashire Transport of Merchandise Committee with the object of fostering the idea among local industrialists. Although it might have been supposed that the railways would not have looked favourably upon such a scheme, the SLT was nevertheless able to reach agreement with the Great Central to book both passengers and goods by tram from Leigh to St Helens, Wigan, Manchester and other places, the GCR perhaps seeing this as a means of penetrating the territory of its rivals.

In Liverpool the concept of goods by tram found a proponent in the Tramway Manager C. R. Bellamy, who as early as 1904 was expounding his views to the Municipal Tramways Association. Looking back into history, he perceived that the Tramways Act of 1870 had already provided for the carriage of general merchandise, but in practice very little advantage had been taken of this provision. Now, under municipal control and with electric lines being extended to connect one town with another, he envisaged that freight traffic could not only prove a welcome source of additional revenue, but would be beneficial to traders in the areas concerned.

Although the Light Railways Act of 1896 had aimed to secure a system of cheap local transport where the railways were not suited to the purpose,

Bellamy saw that the rise of electric tramways now offered new possibilities:
'The ever-increasing network of municipal tramways, with their connecting links, might quickly provide the whole country with a system cheaper in operation than was contemplated under the Light Railway Act, which would do much under proper recognition of its capacity to largely increase the trade and revenue of the country.'

Such a system would, of course, deal only with light consignments of goods on a local basis, but this was a type of traffic which the railways could not adequately cater for, but which was nevertheless of considerable importance to many traders and manufacturers requiring prompt delivery to towns or docks, or indeed to the railways themselves. Bellamy quoted the analogy suggested by an American electric railway operator, that a tramway goods system was 'as flexible as an elephant's trunk', and quite as capable of picking up small things; it could flourish 'on the crumbs that a steam railway would despise', and he believed the railways would welcome the electric tramways as allies.

Any scheme of this nature in an area such as Merseyside and South Lancashire would have emphasised the need for some kind of overall authority to control the services, since the fragmentation of a system under numerous operators (as was the case with the existing passenger tramways) would have presented serious obstacles to the free flow of traffic on which the success of the scheme would have depended. This problem was identified in a paper presented to the Municipal Tramways Association in 1916 by G. W. Holford and W. Clough, Tramways Managers of Salford and Bury respectively; they foresaw the need for some kind of regional joint board:
'If the transport of merchandise over certain areas could be dealt with under one board or organisation there is no doubt that many of the grievances that at present exist would be removed, and many facilities and benefits would follow, but whether such a system could be introduced is a matter for the consideration of the whole of the interested parties in the several areas.'

After examining the criteria required for satisfactory goods operation, and detailing the few instances where freight working on tramways was already being carried out (in Burnley, Glasgow, Huddersfield and Leeds, albeit on a limited scale) the joint authors of the paper concluded that some kind of scheme in Lancashire, involving the conveyance of goods between towns some distance apart, could prove remunerative 'under certain conditions'.

They summarised their views as follows:
'*That* there should be no difficulties in the way of interchange of goods traffic over various undertakings, as the interchange of passenger traffic under like conditions has already proved capable of easy and smooth working.

'*That* the work should be undertaken by a joint board representing the several tramway undertakings interested.'

These conclusions of course epitomised two major problems any such scheme would have encountered. Certainly the interchange of passengers was easy enough, but this was no true analogy, as Manchester's Tramways Manager J. M. McElroy had pointed out: 'Passengers collect and deliver themselves; they walk to the tramway and they walk away. But with goods, there is need for terminals and collection and delivery facilities.' Sidings and depots would have been required, since it could hardly have been envisaged that freight-carrying cars should have simply stood in the middle of the street while their loads were manhandled from one car to another, while a considerable amount of labour would have been called for to deal with the physical interchanges as well as the associated collection and delivery. All this would not only have contributed to costs (and any such project appeared to be no more than marginally profitable at best) but would have interposed delay while freight transfer took place (and speed of delivery was advocated as one of the advantages of the service). The problem of a unified form of control to organise and work the system was less simple of solution. In both Liverpool and Manchester the idea of a coordinated transport organisation was discussed on and off over a period of many years, but no such organisation came into being during the tramway era.

Meanwhile, further meetings were taking place from time to time to discuss the freight plans, with various changes of emphasis. In 1912, for example, a paper was read at a meeting in Oldham of the Lancashire and Cheshire Tramway Managers Association; this examined the possibility of using tramways to carry cotton from the docks of the Manchester Ship Canal to the mills in Oldham and the surrounding district. However, in each case the problem of handling seemed to be capable of no easy solution; every mill would have needed a special siding of its own, with the expense of installation and maintenance of trackwork.

Householders along the routes might not have taken kindly to sleepless nights caused by the passing of a succession of nocturnal freight trams, although it was argued that an electric car passing swiftly by on its smooth rails would cause less disturbance than a slow-moving horse-drawn lorry bumping over the granite setts. It was urged that the adoption of tramway freight operation would indeed reduce the number of heavy road vehicles using the streets, thus not only contributing to the reduction of noise but also relieving

Above: The approach to Pier Head about 1904; the background to car No 216 is formed by the Overhead Railway, beneath which a stream of horse-drawn wagons carries the docks traffic. Some of this traffic could have been handled by electric tramway if schemes of the time had reached fruition. *H. G. Dibdin*

Below: Rice Lane, Walton, in the days when only a few horse-drawn wagons enjoyed the wide expanse of roadway; freight-carrying tramcars could have taken some of their loads through Walton from the docks to inland Lancashire. Here white first class car No 527, inward bound for Lord Street, caters for a different type of traffic. *R. Brook*

congestion and cutting down wear and tear on the road surfaces.

An interesting — if perhaps implausible — scheme put forward in 1913 by Liverpool's Tramways Manager C. W. Mallins envisaged the construction of about 10 miles of new tramways exclusively for the carriage of freight to and from the city's docks. The new lines would have run through the city to connect with the Prescot route, which was the only line giving access to the inland Lancashire network. Such was the density of passenger traffic that Mallins believed it would have been quite impracticable to have operated any worthwhile freight service over the existing tramways within the city area.

The more northerly of his two proposed lines would have left the Alexandra Docks at Bootle via Millon Bridge, Balliol Road and Breeze Hill, and continued through Walton Village and West Derby to join the Prescot tramway at Knotty Ash. The second route would have made its way from Brunswick Dock via Hill Street and Upper Hill Street, Selborne Street and Earle Road to Rathbone Road, to join the Prescot route at Old Swan. The Mersey Docks and Harbour Board's dockside railway would have been electrified; or, if the Board did not like this idea, a new electric tramway would be constructed in the streets paralleling the Board's railway, with suitable connections into the docks.

Given such a system, Mallins contended that it would prove practicable to operate a service of electric freight trains, each consisting of a motor car and two trailers. Such a train would have a capacity of 25 tons of goods, and a 10-minute service would run on each of the two lines. This would enable more than $2\frac{1}{2}$ million tons of goods to be conveyed annually between the docks and the city boundary at Knotty Ash, where it was envisaged that a suitable 'gridiron' and sorting depot would be constructed for the transfer of the traffic to the Prescot Light Railway and the SLT's tracks for onward transmission to the rest of the tramway network. At most, 36 motor cars and 72 trailers would be needed.

The cost of the project would have amounted to a fairly formidable sum: more than £150,000 to electrify the docks railway, about £90,000 for the construction of the two new routes, and a modest £22,000 for the 14 motors and 28 trailers with which a start could be made to establish the service (the remainder of the rolling stock could be purchased later when traffic built up). Other incidentals brought the total capital expenditure required to more than £270,000. Nevertheless, it was reckoned that a profit of some £15,000 a year could be anticipated.

The case for the new system was based on the perennial complaint that existing facilities were inadequate, a view already current in the days of the canals and the Liverpool & Manchester Railway. Mallins pointed out that the tonnage entering and leaving the port of Liverpool had risen from five million tons in 1882 to nearly 36 million tons in 1912, and this increase 'appears to have overburdened the resources of the transport facilities', resulting in slow deliveries, inconvenience and loss, and high charges. 'The great carrying companies find themselves unable to cope satisfactorily with the ever-increasing dock traffic, and it therefore follows that if the Liverpool tramway system could be made to assist in dealing with this congestion, it would indeed play a useful part'.

Effects would be felt over a wide area. From the city boundary at Knotty Ash, traffic would be handed over to the SLT not only to destinations in South Lancashire, but 'by building a certain length of tramways connection could be established with several Yorkshire towns which are connected by various tramway systems'. Thus from Rochdale's Summit terminus, another eight miles would enable a junction to be made at Hebden Bridge with the Halifax Corporation tracks, which in turn met those of Huddersfield, Bradford and Leeds. The problem in Yorkshire, of course, was that the tracks were of different gauges, but it was believed that 'this difficulty could be surmounted by certain mechanical arrangements'.

An alternative way round the gauge problem was the adoption of the trackless trolley system. The trolleybus or 'trackless' was already establishing itself for passenger traffic, and Mallins had been informed 'by certain of the promoters of the trackless trolley system that it is quite practicable for the transport of goods'. The installation of comparable trackless facilities would cost only about £100,000, or little more than one-third of that required for the freight tramways. Not only would it be cheaper in first cost, but it would also prove equally efficient and could well be more flexible; however, before coming to a decision, he 'would require the promoters to demonstrate to his satisfaction the practicability of the system in actual working'. Such an occasion never arose in Liverpool, and neither the freight tramways nor the trackless were to materialise; perhaps not surprisingly, the Harbour Board evinced little enthusiasm, and the concept was fated to be overlain by other developments.

A realistic view of the commercial potential of any such scheme was taken by E. H. Edwardes, general manager of the SLT, the company which had earlier been an enthusiastic advocate. Edwardes concluded that 'the small amount of tonnage handled in a mill or factory during 12 months would not pay the interest and sinking fund in connection with the erection of a siding for the carriage of goods into every mill'. Nevertheless, he saw no reason why central depots or yards should not be established in the manufacturing areas;

goods would be transported by tram to these depots, from which the mills could collect them in their own vehicles, a proceeding which appeared to nullify much of the benefit of the project.

It was Manchester's tramways manager H. M. McElroy who called attention to the important development which had been taking place during the years when they had been discussing the idea (when, as he put it, 'there had been a maximum of talking and a minimum of doing'). Now it seemed to be finally assured that such a scheme would never come into being: 'the introduction of the petrol, steam and electric vehicle has so revolutionised matters that we shall have to hesitate very much before saying that tramways can be generally used for carrying goods.'

In short, they had already hesitated too long, and now the motor lorry had come upon the scene, taking on the tasks the freight-carrying electric cars might have performed.

Not that the motor had yet conquered all. More than 10,000 horse-drawn vehicles brought their loads to and from the Liverpool docks, and for long many of them continued to plod along the docks road almost nose to tail, providing as economical a service as the motor lorry. Their steady average speed of $2\frac{1}{2}$mph kept everything else down to that speed, while frustrated motor drivers acquired the habit of driving up side streets, to run along a parallel road before turning back to the dock road again nearer their destination.

Below: Could the 'trackless trolley' have been used for freight haulage? Perhaps it could have followed the South Lancashire company's route on which this Roe-bodied Guy No 6 of 1930 vintage is leaving St Helens for Atherton. *C. Carter*

# 3 Stations and Suburbs

## The Role of the Railways

*Owing to the excellent railway system in and around Liverpool, enormous residential districts have grown up all about it on both sides of the River Mersey, and the traffic, both daily and holiday, has assumed colossal proportions.*
The Railway Magazine, 1898

Writing in *Our Railways* at the turn of the century, John Pendleton described Liverpool's great stations as 'centres of bustling life' and marvelled that 'scarcely a day passes without the reminder that the city by the Mersey is not only the English but the Continental portal to the New World'. While the ocean liner expresses in their glory were the pride of the line, each of the main termini had its own character and its own pattern of services, both short and long distance, and often highly competitive with those of its neighbours.

Lime Street station 'stands amid very imposing surroundings and tries to live up to them', *The Railway Magazine* wrote in 1905. Certainly the station was a worthy edifice, well situated in the most dignified part of the city, and enthusiastic newspapers compared the 'train shed' with Westminster Hall, concluding that it was in fact bigger. Up to 500 trains a day were dealt with and a staff of nearly 500 were employed. Moreover it was the 'premier' station; not only was it the Merseyside terminus of the LNWR, the self-styled 'Premier Line', but it was the first major terminal in the city. Opened in 1836, Lime Street formed the conclusion of the pioneer Liverpool & Manchester Railway. At first, trains had terminated at Edge Hill because people had wanted to keep the railway from disfiguring the city; but so inconvenient had this arrangement become with the increase in traffic, that an extension had been built, down through a steeply inclined tunnel, into Lime Street. For nearly another 30 years no locomotive had got into Lime Street, for trains were worked by cable on the incline. The situation of the terminus at the end of the tunnel, though impressive enough from the outside, was by no means ideal from the operational point of view; the site was cramped, there was no room to store spare coaches or even to shunt the trains, and the severe gradient formed an obstacle to outgoing trains. Nevertheless, it was to be a long time before the tunnels were opened out and the station expanded.

When Lime Street station was first opened you could have reached London by rail in about 15 hours; by 1900 the best LNWR trains were covering the $193\frac{1}{2}$ miles to Euston in $4\frac{1}{4}$ hours at an average speed of just over 45mph, a sedate pace which the LNWR regarded as befitting the dignified clientele of the Premier Line. On the typical weekday you had a choice of 13 trains, which between them embodied the lavish facilities which the railways were offering in the full enthusiasm of what was to prove their golden age; three of the trains included dining cars, one train had a luncheon car, one had drawing room cars and one was made up of sleeping cars.

Something of the economics of contemporary train operation in an era of cheap labour can be gleaned from a closer look at one particular train: the 4.5pm from Lime Street, due at Euston at 8.20 on a summer evening in 1900. Hauled by a 2-4-0 'Jumbo', it included in its make-up the latest LNWR bogie stock, with one of the massive 12-wheel diners. As well as the guard, the train staff included an attendant, four waiters, a chef and an assistant cook; this happy band of eight ministered to the safety and comfort of a total of just 99 passengers, of whom 18 travelled first class, 19 second class, and the remaining 62 third class. Fourteen of the 'firsts' took dinner at 3s 6d apiece ($17\frac{1}{2}$p) while only 34 of the second- and third-class passengers took their segregated lower-class dinner at 2s 6d a time ($12\frac{1}{2}$p).

An impressive acceleration was made in 1905 with a 3hr 35min schedule from Lime Street to Euston, with only the inevitable stop at Edge Hill; not only was the $192\frac{1}{4}$ miles from Edge Hill to Euston the longest non-stop run on the LNWR, but this became the fastest train to operate between the two cities. By 1938 the fastest time had been brought down to 3hr 15min by the 'Liverpool Flyer'. Another famous train was the 'Merseyside Express', named in 1927; this left Liverpool at 10 in the morning, the return working departing from Euston at 6.05 in the evening, and even this express retained the traditional Southport through coaches which were attached or detached at Lime Street. At the head of the train in the early 1930s could be seen a 'Claughton' or a 'Royal Scot', while the departure from Lime Street was aided by the banker in the shape of an ex-LNWR 0-6-2 'coal tank'. To further the convenience of the Liverpool businessman, the Express invariably made an extra stop at suburban

Right: The railways make their mark: (above) the original Tithebarn Street station in Liverpool; (below) the imposing frontage of the LNWR's hotel at Lime Street station, 'it has a noble elevation and its interior decorations are carried out in the style of the French Renaissance', wrote an Edwardian admirer. At that time you could get a single room for the night for 4s (20p) and 'a plain breakfast' for 1s 6d (7½p).

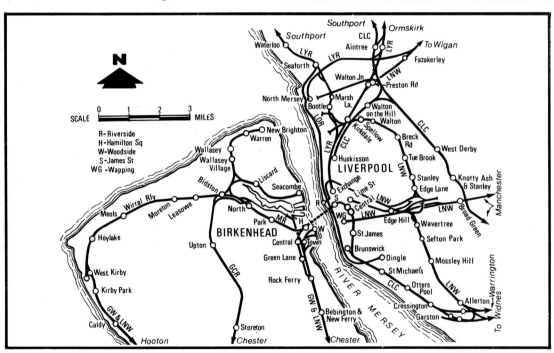

Left: A type long familiar on the rails of Liverpool: an ex-LNWR 0-6-2 'coal tank' blows off steam while awaiting its next turn of duty at Lime Street in 1932. Among their functions these engines banked up the steep climb to Edge Hill.  *W. B. Stocks*

Above: The approach to Liverpool Central station: ghost-like in its white livery, first class car No 484 passes horse-drawn cabs on its way to Pier Head.  *R. Brook*

Below: Liverpool's Exchange: apotheosis of L&YR motive power, a Hughes 4-6-0 heads an express while its crew pose for the photographer. A line of waiting horse-drawn cabs can be seen on the extreme left.
*Ian Allan Library*

Top left: A Liverpool-Manchester 'Punctual' express passes Halewood in 1906 hauled by GCR 4-4-0 No 877, a 7-footer of 1899. The train of five GCR bogie coaches includes vehicles in the livery with cream upper panels. *Ian Allan Library*

Centre left: CLC Liverpool-Manchester train hauled by 4-4-0 No 1016, including a mixed assortment of vans and six-wheel coaches in GCR days. *Ian Allan Library*

Bottom left: GCR No 1016 again Manchester-bound, this time on bogie stock, including coaches built by the GNR. *Ian Allan Library*

Top: Early post-grouping days on the CLC; LNER No 858, an ex-GCR Pollitt 4-4-0 of 1899, takes a Liverpool-Manchester train including GNR-built stock. *Ian Allan Library*

Above: Wirral excursion: LNER C13 class 4-4-2T No 5190 takes water at Neston & Parkgate when working a Sunday excursion from Seacombe to Caergwrle Castle in 1934. Note the six-wheel coach. *Ian Allan Library*

As well as the longer-distance trains, notable services were those of the rival routes between Liverpool and Manchester; the LNWR had the easiest and slightly shorter way (32 miles) but the Cheshire Lines prided itself on maintaining the reputation of its 'Punctual' expresses. Contrast in motive power is provided by above, the LNWR's 'Experiment' 4-6-0 (No 2626 *Chillington* of 1909 is seen here) and below, the Great Central's Pollitt 4-4-0s (such as No 270 of 1898 seen at Halewood) which continued to flourish until well into LNER days. *Ian Allan Library*

Mossley Hill to pick up before speeding Londonwards. Suburban traffic from Lime Street, perhaps not so prolific as from its rival termini, included the branch to Bootle (which surprisingly retained a local passenger service until as late as 1948) as well as residential trains to such suburbs as Sefton Park and Wavertree on the Crewe line, and Huyton and Rainhill on the Manchester line.

The Cheshire Lines' Liverpool Central, opened in 1874, had replaced the old Brunswick Street station which was then relegated to goods traffic only. Again a tunnel (the longest on the CLC) was needed to bring the line into the new central location. More tunnels came later, to carry the Mersey Railway's trains into their low-level terminus beneath the CLC station in 1892. Exchange, the Lancashire & Yorkshire Railway's ten-platform terminus, completed the city's semi-circle of main-line stations, each owned by a different company in pre-Grouping days, and each offering services to many of the same places as its rivals.

Outstanding among these competitive services were the routes to Manchester; you could go to Cottonopolis from any of the three Liverpool termini, travelling in each case on a fast train making the journey in about 40 minutes. Each took a different route of different length, and of course each company intimated that its own service was the best. All round, they were not far wrong, for taken together there was the equivalent of a fast train between the two cities every 20 minutes throughout the day. The Great Central, for example, advertised itself on the CLC route as the 'Punctual Service', and its speedy light-weight trains were among the last duties of single-driver locomotives, its 4-2-2s working alongside smaller varieties of 4-4-0s until well into the 1920s. In 1925 'Single' No 5972 enjoyed an extra brief moment of glory when it took part in the centenary procession of historic locomotives at the Stockton & Darlington celebrations, before returning to its still-normal role of handling Liverpool-Manchester expresses. Neverthe-less in the early post-Grouping era, 'strangers' began to appear, such as ex-Great Northern Atlantics while Gresley 'J39' 0-6-0s were seen on goods trains on the CLC.

The 45-minute service had started as early as 1877, from which time the Sacre 'Singles' of the Manchester, Sheffield & Lincolnshire Railway had built up the reputation for timekeeping. During the Edwardian heyday, their successors the GCR 'Singles' and 4-4-0s maintained the tradition, a link of ten locomotives each making two round journeys in the course of their day's duty and so notching up a total of 136 miles a day — an interesting insight into the degree of intensity of motive power utilisation at this period. Almost half of Liverpool Central's daily business of about 85 arrivals and departures were routed over the Manchester line; the 45-minute expresses included a one-minute inter-mediate stop at Warrington, though a few trains were booked to cover the ground in 40 minutes by making use of avoiding lines to bypass Warrington.

The LNWR's route to Manchester was the easiest, apart from the 1¾-mile climb up to Edge Hill, and it was also the shortest at just 32 miles compared with 34 miles on the CLC and 37 miles on the LYR. At the start of the century the LNWR's trains were typically made up of half a dozen bogie coaches, described as 'fitted with steam heating apparatus and electric light-ing, and in fact thoroughly up to date in every respect'. Those whose business required them to commute daily to Manchester could obtain an annual season ticket for £25 12s (£25.60) first class.

To justify the apparent over-abundance of trains on the three main routes, it was generally pointed out that in fact they served different places on the way, a claim seemingly at variance with the operators' insistence on the speed and punctuality of their respective through trains. However, there was no denying some weight in the contention; in any case, rationalisation would not have been easy, at least not until the railways as a whole were in such a plight as to call for the attentions of a Beeching.

In its own favour the L&YR could contend that its service from Liverpool Exchange was convenient for passengers who lived along its Southport electrified line and who wanted to get to Manchester as expeditiously as possible. It would have been incon-venient if they had had to transfer to Lime Street, to which there was no direct tram service from Exchange. As for other passengers, Exchange was closer to the central business district than Lime Street. For its part the CLC could equally claim the advantageous pos-ition of its Central station, a situation matched by the favourable location of its Manchester Central. Moreover its Liverpool terminus, fed directly by the Mersey Railway, provided direct connection for passengers to and from Birkenhead and the Wirral peninsula.

As for concentrating the traffic on to the 'best' route, neither Lime Street nor Central appeared to have sufficient spare capacity to absorb the extra load. Lime Street's cramped site was already overcrowded, while Central's narrow approaches were also intensively used for freight as well as passenger traffic. Electrification was a possible solution to the problem of increasing capacity, but this was not to become a reality for the Manchester routes.

Liverpool to Southport was another duplicated route; the obvious way of course was on the L&YR, where from 1904 a fast and frequent electrified service operated over the 18½ miles. The CLC offered an alternative, though this amounted to no less than 31

'Royal Scot' motive power on Liverpool-London expresses: (top) No 6140 'Hector' on the 10.30am from Euston in 1929; (above) in the summer of 1932 No 6140 again, now fitted with smoke deflectors, heads the first run of the accelerated 5.25pm from Liverpool to London, to make the journey in 3hr 20min as one of the fastest trains on the LMS.
*Real Photographs*

Overground and Underground on Merseyside.

Above: a quiet moment at Pier Head, usually one of the busiest stations on the Liverpool Overhead Railway. This view shows the layout of the station on its viaduct; note the crossover. *Real Photographs*

Centre : a 3-car Mersey Railway train rounds the curve into Birkenhead Central. The American style of the early clerestory-roofed cars is obvious; note the white upper panels indicating the first-class saloon on the leading car. *W. Hubert Foster*

Bottom : Great Central 4-4-2 tanks worked local trains on the CLC lines in the Liverpool area. *Ian Allan Library*

39

miles and practically boxed the compass in the course of its wanderings; from Central it proceeded southwards to Garston and Hunts Cross before venturing north via the 'belt' line through the eastern outskirts of the city, and then roughly paralleling the LYR route to its own station in Southport. Though not obviously attractive to the through passenger, the CLC line carried a useful amount of local traffic in the Liverpool suburban area. Although the service to Walton-on-the-Hill ended in 1917, as late as the 1920s new stations were opened at Clubmoor and Warbreck to stimulate the suburban traffic, though by this time it was probably too late to stem the flow to tram and bus.

The railways had indeed done much to encourage the development of suburban traffic. As early as the 1850s the East Lancashire Railway (later part of the L&YR) was offering free first-class season tickets to those who built houses with a rateable value of at least £50 a year in the areas of Aintree, Maghull, Town Green, Ormskirk or Burscough. The farther out you went, the longer the period covered by your free season: only seven years at Aintree, but you got no less than 18 years free travel if you settled at Burscough.

One of the institutions of the period was the Sunday School outing, and the railways offered their services to those contemplating the organisation of such excursions. The LNWR, for example, published a booklet containing suggestions for suitable locations for picnics: 'the LNWR offers to the promoters of Liverpool Sunday School outings a fine field for selection, including Mossley Hill (for Calderstones Park), Roby (for Roby Park), Allerton, Hale Bank (for Hale), Frodsham (for Overton Hills), Chester, and a number of other places, to say nothing of Southport, the charms of which are well known and deservedly popular.' Details of fares and catering were listed, while if the normal train services proved unsuitable for the occasion, the company were willing to put on a special train, provided the party consisted of not less than 300 people. But as much of a handful as 300 lively youngsters may have appeared to harassed Sunday School organisers, their number pales into insignificance beside the 1,600 Lever Brothers employees who enjoyed a two-day excursion to the Paris Exhibition in 1900. Four 'Sunlight Soap' special trains took this mammoth party out from Bebington on a Friday afternoon, two of the trains bound for Dover and the other two for Folkestone to meet the cross-channel ferries. The return was made on Saturday night, with arrival back at Birkenhead on Sunday afternoon to complete a memorable outing in the days when Continental travel for the masses was still far in the future.

More modest in extent was some of the pleasure

traffic handled at Liverpool Central. There were racegoers to Aintree, for example, while Mersey Road station served the nearby Aigburth cricket ground where some of the county matches were played. Winter saw skaters thronging Sefton meadows when ice covered the flooded fields, and on at least one chilly day as many as 2,000 skaters left Central for this venue.

Perhaps less fortunate in earlier times was the relationship of St Helens to its railway facilities. Left unserved by the Liverpool & Manchester trunk line, the town was afforded a direct link with Merseyside with the opening of the line to Huyton in 1871, but while some workmen's traffic developed from St Helens and Thatto Heath to Prescot and Liverpool, St Helens Junction continued as the station for the main Liverpool-Manchester route. North-west of St Helens, in the mainly agricultural area extending to Southport, the early years of the 20th century saw the introduction of steam rail-motors on several services by the LYR in an attempt to provide economical operation on sparsely-trafficked lines; in 1906 rail-motors were put on between St Helens and Rainford and Ormskirk, as well as between Southport and Ormskirk, and Southport and Barton. New 'halts' were built at the same time; these included Heys Crossing, White Moss Crossing and Westhead on the Rainford Junction-Ormskirk line.

By the early years of the new century electric tramways were abstracting traffic from the local railways in cases where distances were short and the competing tramcars frequent, convenient and cheap; it was probably less than coincidental that the rail fare for the somewhat circuitous $7\frac{1}{2}$ miles from Alexandra Dock, Bootle, to Lime Street was only 2d (less than 1p). The railways countered the threat, and won back some of the lost ground, by offering better services including generous season ticket rates and better trains. At the same time they capitalised on their advantage of higher speed by cultivating traffic to and from localities beyond the reach of the tramways.

The LNWR, for example, retained a healthy local traffic on its line to Crewe, while the L&YR in 1907 opened three new 'halts' (the word was still sufficiently novel in this context for the press to put it in inverted commas) on the Aintree and Ormskirk line, at Orrell Park, at Old Roan and at Aughton Park; at first these were served by steam rail motors, and later, after electrification, they were transformed into full-scale stations. On the Southport line, the L&YR in 1908 was extending the station and facilities at Ainsdale with the intention of fostering a new residential district to bring more commuters to its trains.

As a consequence of the improvement of services, including electrification, many of the railways in the Liverpool area were able to retain a useful share of

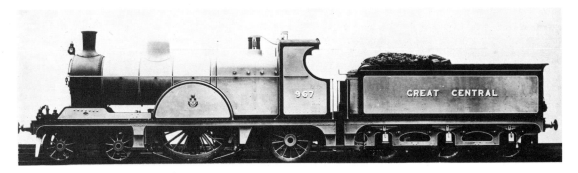

Above and right: Great Central motive power on CLC services into Liverpool Central included Pollitt 'singles', such as No 967 (above) built in 1900 with 7ft 9in driving wheels. Local services in the area (and on the GCR Seacombe line) were long the haunts of the Robinson 4-4-2T (right) No 359 was one of a class dating from 1903-5 with 5ft 7in coupled wheels. *Ian Allan Library*

Below: The graceful GCR 'singles' were still giving good service on the Cheshire Lines Liverpool- Manchester 'Punctual' expresses into the 1920s, by which time they were among the last single-driver locomotives still in action. Here 4-2-2 No 967 is caught in full flight near Halewood in GCR days. *Ian Allan Library*

traffic even into the age of the motor car and bus, with the result that the rail network continued to play a more positive role in the Merseyside region than in some other conurbations. Even some of the less promising lines remained open until a surprisingly late date; the former CLC's roundabout Southport service, for example, continued until 1952 when it was cut back to Aintree, while the Gateacre service survived as late as 1972 to become the last to use the Liverpool Central terminus. Indeed, more recent years have seen a resurrection of part of the line, with electrification to Garston.

Rail facilities in central Liverpool nevertheless suffered the disadvantage, which they shared with more than one other city, of having several termini with no connecting link across the city. In Liverpool's case, there was no connection to give a north to south route between Exchange and Central, though again it is one of the surprising aspects of the continuing rail legacy that such a connection was made much later in the shape of the Merseyrail 'Link'. Again, there was no through east to west connection, the River Mersey forming an effective barrier. True, there was the Mersey Railway, but for Liverpool this remained of essentially local significance, even though its scope was extended by its linking with the Wirral lines on electrification, and much later by the construction of the 'Loop' to provide better interchange in central Liverpool.

The idea of an underground railway system received attention from time to time. At the start of the 1930s, for example, the Liverpool city authorities were considering a scheme for an underground which would have provided a loop connecting Exchange, Central and Lime Street. It was contended that such a line would greatly improve traffic circulation within the city centre and improve interchange facilities between the three termini. Moreover, the work involved in its construction would have helped to relieve local unemployment.

Tube railways were not destined to receive the support of Liverpool's Transport Manager of the 1930s, W. G. Marks, who saw their capital costs as ruling them out as a practical proposition for his city 'Liverpool is no mean city', he said, 'but what sort of a capital expenditure will be required for a system of underground railways in a city of any reasonable size?' Liverpool had 86 route miles to tramways to provide suitable transport facilities for the public, and 'I cannot see how we are going to give the public anything like good facilities with less than half the present service coupled with underground railways'. Not only would the cost of such railways mean higher fares, but passengers would have a less accessible system; they would have to walk to the station and descend to the trains, whereas the tramcar could be boarded almost anywhere. Marks did not believe that underground railways would be financially viable in Liverpool; on the contrary, 'they would be a constant drain on the rates'. Nevertheless, a later age of greater congestion and coordination saw the facilities of the pioneer electric lines extended across the city by Merseyrail 'Loop' and 'Link' as well as augmented by further suburban electrification.

## The Southport Corridor

*The Lancashire & Yorkshire Railway had not gone into the work of electrification to save money, but to make money.*
John A. F. Aspinall, General Manager, L&YR, 1909

Far from the noise of the docks and the congestion of the city, the lower shore of the Mersey offered tempting prospects for those who could afford a suburban retreat. Already by the early years of the 19th century neat villas dotted the coastline past Waterloo and Crosby, where Liverpool merchants established themselves in style, commuting daily to and from the great port by coach, omnibus or fast packet boat on the Leeds & Liverpool Canal. Farther north yet, the town of Southport had grown from almost literally nothing to become a favourable resort and residential area by the end of the century. With its blend of suburban, residential and holiday traffic, this 'Southport corridor' held out bright prospects to the L&YR, whose thoughts turned to the creation of one of the earliest major electrification projects, to facilitate the working of this busy 18-mile 'main line' from Liverpool Exchange to Southport.

As a symbol of its newly-attained adulthood, Southport had already obtained its first tramways in 1873, when the Southport Tramways Company started operation, followed in 1880 by a second company, the Birkdale & Southport. The Corporation bought out the first company and proceeded to electrify, its own electric cars starting to run in 1900. Although the Birkdale & Southport's lines were bought by the Corporation in that year, the company still continued to operate until 1918, when it too was finally acquired by the Corporation, when its territory was incorporated into the County Borough of Southport. A few years later came a further advance to keep in line with modern transport, when the first municipal motor bus service was started in 1924.

Southport could claim to be second only to Blackpool in its attractions as a resort, and before World War 1 the height of the season witnessed more than 200 trains a day, both ordinary and special, pulling into the town's several stations to unload their crowds of holidaymakers and excursionists, predominantly

Above: Horse-car days in Southport: No 18 carries a liberal display of destinations (Birkdale, Hesketh Park, Churchtown, Botanic Gardens — where, a placard in the window tells us, there is a band performance this afternoon — and Cheshire Lines Railway) though business is obviously slack at the moment. If you do not care to travel by tramcar, you can visit Timberlake of Neville Street, who is advertising Bicycles, Tricycles, Bassinettes and Mail Carts. *R. Brook*

Centre left: The crew of Southport Corporation open-top car No 14 pose at the Kew Gardens terminus in 1912. *R. Brook*

Bottom left: Early days on Southport Corporation's motor buses: a rural scene at Woodvale in 1926 as Vulcan No 4 is cranked up, while a double-decker of Waterloo & Crosby Motor Services pulls out to overtake. *C. Carter*

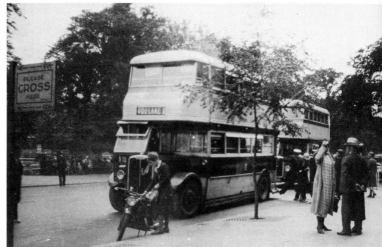

Top right: Southport's Lord Street in 1929: the crew of Titan No 10, the first Leyland bus to be acquired by the Corporation, await departure time on the service to Crossens. *Ian Allan Library*

Centre right: Lord Street in the early 1930s: Southport Corporation double-deck Vulcan No 13 prepares to depart for Roe Lane. *C. Carter*

Below: The select setting of the Birkdale tramways: in leafy York Road, the private motor car is already in evidence, perhaps owned by one of the Liverpool businessmen the L&YR encouraged as commuters on its Southport electric trains. *R. Brook*

from the industrial towns of inland Lancashire. The L&YR's posters beamed down upon you throughout its territory, proclaiming that 'Southport's Sunshine and Salubrious Sea Air Stimulate and Strengthen'. As a contemporary description put it, Southport is 'a splendid centre for recuperation; it is quieter than Blackpool, but provides nearly as many attractions, while its gardens and other features recommend it as a permanent place of residence.' It was indeed especially this 'permanent place of residence' that the L&YR was to encourage as the basis of the prosperity of its electric line.

For the benefit of those venturing from the deep south, through coaches were worked to Southport from London. The LNWR carried them on its 12.25 and 2.40pm trains from Euston, and special fares offered good value to those who fancied a taste of the northern lights and sea breezes. 'Tourist' tickets were issued at 32s 9d (£1.64) and 'Weekend' tickets at 20s 9d (£1.04). A cheap excursion also left London on Friday night at a return fare of only £1, while at certain times there was a bargain-rate 'Special' for no more than 17s (85p).

A contemporary description of this 'salubrious coast town' at the turn of the century recalls the fact that the L&YR by no means had a monopoly in rail services:
'The CLC station in Lord Street adjoins the Winter Gardens and Opera House, which is the chief centre of attraction for the town, and affords a varied round of entertainment at all seasons of the year. From this station express trains perform the journey to Liverpool and Manchester within the hour.'

The Cheshire Lines railway came in along the coast, having forsaken the inland meadows and crossed the coastwise LYR line to run through the Ainsdale Hills and the Birkdale Hills parallel with the sea: appropriately a new station named 'Seaside' was opened in 1901. The line then curved round into the town to end up fronting Lord Street, where the Liverpool train concluded its journey facing in almost the same direction as it had started at Liverpool Central.

But while the two companies were rival suitors for the hand of the Southport visitor, the L&YR had the advantage of a much shorter route with a much greater traffic potential. The L&YR decided on electrification not only to Southport, but further along the Preston line as far as Crossens, effectively a suburb of the seaside resort and a distance of 22 miles from Liverpool Exchange. The work was carried out remarkably speedily; orders were placed in the autumn of 1902 and the first trial runs on the newly electrified lines were made at the end of December in the following year. Public services started in March 1904, though it was some little time before the last of the

steam trains were entirely superseded.

In an address to the Institution of Locomotive Engineers in 1909, the L&YR's General Manager John Aspinall expounded his philosophy of railway electrification in the age of the electric tramway:
'In a district where a railway has had its tracks paralleled by tramways running for some distance from the terminal of a great city, the creation of an electric railway service will have the immediate effect of bringing back to the line of railway large numbers of those passengers who have used the trams in the early stages of their construction, but who find that they cannot tolerate the great waste of time which results from the very slow speed and the many stops due to the crowded streets through which the trams have to run.

'It must, however, be remembered that unless an electrified railway can be continued for some distance so as to earn a good average fare, stations which are close together and but a short distance from the great city will yield very low fares without giving any opportunity of picking up the ever-recurring penny paid by the short-distance traveller on the trams.'

The sphere of the electric railway, he asserted, was to be found in those areas beyond the influence of the local tramways:
'The main object should be to induce a large number of people who have business in the towns to live further out, and so bring up the average fare of the railway to such a figure as will make it profitable, leaving the very short distance traffic to the municipal tramways.'

Electrification resulted in economy of operation and made it possible to defer any costly increase in capacity at termini; but, as Aspinall pointed out, the L&YR did not undertake the work of electrification to *save* money, but to *make* money. It was therefore crucial to ensure that the traffic potential existed:
'An increase in speed, coupled with greater frequency of trains, will soon begin in a populous district to yield that flow of traffic which may naturally be expected from such facilities, but it must at once be recognised that higher speeds and more trains cost money. If, therefore, the district is not one in which there is a possibility of a growth of traffic, nothing can be gained.'

So what was the possibility of growth on the Liverpool-Southport line? 'After leaving Liverpool', Aspinall went on, 'all the stations are close to the sea. Many of them are situated in the midst of attractive residential districts, and were thus likely to produce additional traffic if good travelling facilities were provided'. Moreover once the Liverpool area was left

Top right: First class comfort on one of the Lancashire & Yorkshire Railway's early electric trains; first class cars had upholstered seats and mahogany decoration with light wood panelling.

Centre right: The L&YR's Liverpool-Southport electrics won the reputation of being the swiftest in Britain; here an 'express' composed of original stock hurries past the dunes, bound for Liverpool, making the journey as rapidly as the fastest steam express. *W. B. Stocks*

Below: An LMS train of 1940 for the Liverpool-Southport-Ormskirk lines; capable of reaching 70mph, the new stock enabled the schedules to be notably speeded up. The three-car sets comprised motor, third class trailer, and composite driving trailer, while two-car sets were also introduced to give the greatest flexibility in train formation. Like the original stock, they were of the saloon type, but air-operated sliding doors were a feature.
*Ian Allan Library*

behind, traffic on the line was almost entirely passenger; as well as the daily commuter flow into and out of Liverpool morning and evening, there was also a considerable amount of traffic during the day for shopping and other purposes.

As to the new electric service, this 'is considered to be the fastest service of such a character in existence'. Although no change was made in the speed of the expresses which ran between Liverpool and Southport in 25 minutes, the greater acceleration of the electrics (which could reach 30mph in 30 seconds) resulted in a marked improvement in the stopping trains; with 14 intermediate stops these were now scheduled to cover the ground in 37 minutes compared with the 54 minutes taken by the steam trains. Between Liverpool and Hall Road, which was effectively the end of the 'suburban' area, the time was cut from 25 minutes to 17 minutes. Frequency was also improved; the number of trains each way between Liverpool and Southport was increased from 36 to 70 a day, while the number to Hall Road was increased from 36 to 60.

The economy of operation resulting from the more intensive utilisation possible with electric stock is illustrated by the fact that the 30 locomotives and 152 coaches needed to maintain the services in steam days were replaced by only 38 motor cars and 53 trailers.

Much attention was given to the design of the new rolling stock, and Aspinall provides an insight into the philosophy behind the decision to adopt the end-door saloon pattern. The traditional compartment-type coach with its many doors required a larger platform staff to ensure that all the doors were safely closed, while power-operated sliding doors created risks to passengers as well as the possibility of jamming in the event of accident. On the other hand, the use of large end doors, opened and closed by the passengers themselves, reduced the labour force while enabling passengers to move quickly in and out. L&YR experience showed that even a crowded train could be emptied in 50 seconds at a terminus, while stops at intermediate stations occupied no more than 15 seconds. As a further aid to speedy flow, passengers were encouraged to enter a car at the rear door and to alight at the front. The last of the original stock survived until 1942, and while the new 1926 stock which augmented it was of the compartment type, a return to the saloon pattern was made in the 1939 LMS design.

While traffic was developing in a satisfactory manner, the L&YR nevertheless missed no opportunity to publicise the advantages of living on the lines of its electric railways. Under the title *Ideal Residential Districts*, for example, a publicity booklet detailed the character of the various places served, the train facilities and fares, and the 'abundance of accommodation to suit all incomes'. Details were provided of rents, rates and the price of gas, as well as the location of such amenities as golf links, all with the object of guiding 'the Liverpudlian who is contemplating living "further out" or the engaged couple deciding where to commence housekeeping'. Another illustrated booklet entitled *Where to Golf* had the added authority of a foreword by a former Open champion, Harold Hilton. This not only described the links, but of course strongly hinted that the golfer would do well to travel by train: 'Today the Liverpool golfer has, as regards his favourite pastime, an exceptional life of luxury. Take, for instance, the electric train service between Liverpool and Southport. The trains are of amazing frequency, in fact so frequent that a player need not worry as regards the train on the return journey to town.'

Extension of electrification to Aintree in 1906-7 brought a further promising area within the ambit of electric traction. 'The country round Aintree, Walton Junction and Preston Road is suitable in an eminent degree for development as a residential district for the working population engaged in the city and at the docks', commented *Tramway and Railway World*. 'It may be confidently predicted that the erection of residences along this line will be carried on with no less rapidity and enterprise than is evidenced along the entire length of the Southport line'. Aintree was within range of the Corporation tramways, and Aspinall was soon able to report with some satisfaction that 'a very large traffic which was previously taken away by the municipal tramways, which run parallel with and not many yards from the electric line, has now come back to the railway'.

But the L&YR was not content to end its progress at Aintree; following Aspinall's dictum that an electric railway should aim beyond the limits of the tramways, electrification was extended across country, first to Maghull in 1909, then to Town Green in 1911, and to the small town of Ormskirk in 1913, a distance of about 12 miles from Exchange, thus encouraging another corridor of suburban development. At Ormskirk, elderly ladies on the platforms continued to sell gingerbread (a local speciality) while main line trains went on to Preston and steam rail-motors worked the branch to Rainsford. Extension of electric working beyond Ormskirk was contemplated, to complete a second electrified route to Southport, but with the intervention of World War 1 and the subsequent merger of the L&YR with the LNWR and later the LMS, no such scheme reached fruition.

Meanwhile, the L&YR maintained friendly relations with the neighbouring Liverpool Overhead Railway. Cooperation resulted in the construction of connecting links from the LOR's Seaforth Sands station to the L&YR's Seaforth station on the Southport line, and to the L&YR's North Mersey branch to enable through trains to work from the LOR to Aintree. However,

Above: A good idea of the distinctive character of the L&YR Southport electric stock may be gained from this view of a clerestory-roof motor and an elliptical-roof trailer taken in the sidings at Hall Road in 1931. *N. N. Forbes*

Centre right: The L&YR constructed special lightweight cars for the joint working with the Liverpool Overhead Railway between Southport and Dingle. Each car had first and third class accommodation, and a motorman's compartment at each end for working as a single unit.

Bottom right: Grand National Day, and Liverpool Overhead Railway train No 24 of the original stock leaves Linacre Road LMS station on its way to Aintree. *N. N. Forbes*

Above: Race crowds on the L&YR at Aintree in 1910, one of the annual peak problems for the company's electric trains.

Below: Aintree on a race day in 1910; an L&YR electric train, composed of ordinary steam stock flanked by electric motor cars, disgorges its load of racegoers, while a Liverpool Overhead train on one of its annual extensions to Aintree can be seen in the far platform.

before through running between the two railways could become a reality, problems arising from the lack of standardisation had to be overcome. Not for the last time, separate electric lines had gone their own way, with the result that incompatibilities appeared when opposites met. The LOR originally had its conductor rail laid between the running rails, and this had to be changed to the outside position in conformity with the L&YR. And while LOR trains could thus happily traverse L&YR metals, the track of the Overhead was unsuited to the wide and heavy stock of the L&YR, which was obliged to construct new lightweight cars if it was to participate in through running on to its neighbour.

The link between the LOR, from its Seaforth Sands station, to the L&YR at Seaforth and Litherland, was opened on 2 July 1905, thus enabling LOR trains to connect with the L&YR electrics. The L&YR through service from Southport and over the Overhead to Dingle started on 2 February 1906, though it appears to have attracted little support — probably few Liverpool dockers commuted from Southport. Generally no more than a single car ran once an hour, and even this was withdrawn in 1914. Through service also came off the Overhead to Aintree, though latterly this was confined to Grand National days when LOR trains made their annual pilgrimage over the junction and the connecting line amid displays of pyrotechnics from the live rail. Though in some respects spasmodic, cooperation between the Overhead and the Lancashire & Yorkshire represented the first example in Britain of interrunning between two separate electric railways.

The 1907 spring race meeting at Aintree marked a notable occasion for the L&YR, for this was the first time it worked all its special race traffic electrically. Six electric 'specials' were in use to provide a shuttle service to and from Aintree, and they were believed to be the largest and heaviest electric trains ever to have run in Britain; each weighed about 230 tons and had seats for more than 500 passengers. Two of the trains consisted of the ordinary electric stock, but the other four were of decidedly novel formation, for each was made up of a rake of ten of the company's con-

ventional six-wheel coaches with an electric motor car fore and aft; the necessary cables between the two motor cars were carried over the roofs of the train. This unusual make-up continued to do duty on race days for many years.

In addition to the electrics, processions of 'specials' from many parts made their way to Aintree on Grand National day. In the Coronation year of 1911, for example, the LNWR ran six special day excursions from London direct in the morning, departing from Euston between seven and nine o'clock. The company disclosed some interesting figures which recall the opulent days of railway facilities, when labour was cheap and appetites obviously hearty. These six trains required a staff of 60 cooks and 100 attendants to man the restaurant cars, in which they served a total of over 1,000 breakfasts, nearly 200 luncheons, more than 650 teas and nearly 2,000 dinners. Consumed at these meals were 1,500lb of meat and 200lb of ham, 150 chickens, 850lb of fish and 5,000 eggs, washed down by 2,300 bottles of beer and 220 bottles of whisky. Not to be outdone, the Great Central also ran excursions from London, including lunch, tea and dinner served on board. For this round trip the charge (including meals) was £1 16s first class (£1.80) and only £1 third class.

Aintree on race days was a joy to the 'spotter'; apart from the locals, some 60 long-distance specials such as those from London were to be seen, many of them double-headed by a wide variety of locomotives. In the grouping days of the 1920s and 1930s, Gresley Pacifics from the LNER shared tracks with LMS Hughes 4-6-0s and Midland Compounds, while ex-GCR 4-6-0s met LMS '2P' 4-4-0s and Moguls, alongside a range of 0-6-0s. Coaches showed corresponding variety; from the Pullmans of the LNER's special from Kings Cross, to antiquated six-wheelers. Their starting points included not only the London termini (Euston, Kings Cross, St Pancras and Marylebone) but practically all parts of the country, including Glasgow, Carlisle, Newcastle, Northampton and Bristol.

# 4  Tramways and Roadways

## 'Grass Tracks'

*Tramways are unsurpassed for the cheap conveyance of great masses of the population in industrial areas, and they have proved that no other vehicle yet placed upon the road can deal with the peak load traffic in our great cities and industrial areas as economically and efficiently as they do.*

Percy Priestly, General Manager, Liverpool Corporation Tramways, 1926

One of the most striking features of Liverpool's tramway system was the spacious nature of many of its suburban routes, where new tracks had been incorporated into the layout of new suburbs. This feature owed much to the long tradition of planning which enabled both roads and transport services to be integrated into suburban development; in its turn this tradition owed much to the foresight of the Council and its City Engineer, John A. Brodie, who in the years before World War 1 had insisted on the need for roads of adequate width. As a result Liverpool could boast a total of 35 miles of new roads of widths varying from 84ft to 200ft; outstanding among these and anticipating the 'ring road' principle of later years was one of Brodie's inspirations, Queens Drive, begun in 1903 and eventually extending for seven miles through a largely unbuilt area in a semi-circle through Wavertree, West Derby and Walton. Most of the roads were of a standard 120ft width, and consisted of dual carriageways with a central reservation allowing for the installation of tramways on sleeper tracks.

The original intention had been to construct the roads with the tramway in the centre of the carriageway in the normal manner, and this was done in some instances; in part of Menlove Avenue, for example, when built in 1910 to a width of 114ft, the paved tramway was sited in the carriageway. But, with the increase in the amount of motor traffic, as well as the desire for higher speeds, dual carriageways were installed, with the tramways laid on sleeper tracks in the central strip, embellished with grass and with 'protection for straying animals etc provided by low privet hedges and curbs' (a reminder by Brodie of the semi-rural character of some of the outlying routes when they were first built). Perhaps because of their bucolic setting, some scepticism was expressed over the horticultural aspects of the 'grass tracks', but Brodie showed that even this matter had been given attention:

'The grass difficulty is not very serious, but like everything else it requires to be properly tackled and dealt with. There are grasses and grasses; if you put down rye grass you may expect a good crop at the beginning of the season, if you put down grasses of the fescue class in a road you will have a hard grass, good from the point of view of wear, and which will require little or nothing in the way of cutting.'

On stretches where the tramways had not yet been laid, the grass-sown reservations served an unofficial temporary purpose as children's playgrounds.

A bonus for residents along the roads was the quieter running of the cars on the sound-deadening sleeper tracks. Earlier examples of this type of construction had included sections of Aigburth Road in 1921 and part of Menlove Avenue in 1922, both of which were 120ft wide. In some places the old road was retained to form one side of the new dual carriageway.

Brodie enumerated the principles of his planning in a paper he presented to the annual conference of the Tramways and Light Railways Association in 1914. He described some of the points arising in connection with town planning and roads 'which are likely to affect, or to be affected by, the methods adopted for the local conveyance of passengers between the central areas and the districts likely to be town-planned on the outskirts of the larger towns of this country'. Brodie himself had had 30 years' experience in the construction of tramways and street improvements in Liverpool, as well as the responsibility for new housing estates accommodating about 150,000 people.

Among the special problems affecting Liverpool's transport pattern were the River Mersey, which formed a natural barrier to westward communication, and the steep hills in the direction of densely-populated Eyerton to the north-east, which had prevented a direct approach to the undeveloped land just beyond. Until the passing of the Town Planning Act of 1909 there were no general powers for dealing with street improvements, which were dependent on the agreement of landowners and local authorities, with the result that large-scale schemes could not be easily evolved. In Liverpool, however, hitherto separate districts to the south of the city had now been included within the boundaries in order that suitable planning

Top right: Liverpool's broad highways: part of the newly-widened Menlove Avenue near the Calderstones terminus, with first class car No 523. Work undertaken here in 1910 involved widening from 36ft to 114ft, retaining the old road and its established trees on the right. As motor traffic increased, later road projects put tramways on sleeper track on a central reservation. Among detail work may be noted the liver birds on top of the finials of the overhead standards. *N. N. Forbes*

Centre right: The social scene in old Liverpool: tramcar No 351 on the Litherland route passes the Mission Hall, Linacre. The multitude of children and others outside the hall and in the street recall the densely overcrowded conditions which improvements in local transport did much to ameliorate. *H. G Dibdin*

Below: The 'grass track' tramways: where land alongside the road could be purchased cheaply, the tramway could be laid in a separate strip, with resultant economy in construction and maintenance and the potential for higher speed. This is Broad Green Road, looking towards Bowring Park, shortly after the tramway was laid in 1914-15. The park and the new carriageway are on the right, while suburban housing already lines one side of the original road; grass between the rails, and the youthful privet hedges at either side, add to the attraction of the layout. *H. G. Dibdin*

schemes could be drawn up to cover the area as a whole.

As far back as 1867 Liverpool had investigated the need for street improvements, and plans included the construction of a 180ft wide boulevard to encircle the city. Over a period of 50 years about £4 million had been spent on street improvements. Under a special Act of 1908 the Corporation obtained powers to control the width, direction and gradient of main roads, and from then until 1914 about 20 miles of new or widened roads had appeared, mainly on the outskirts of the city. Powers were further augmented by the 1909 Town Planning Act, which had direct bearing on the planning of new suburban areas, the replanning of older areas, the rehousing of the population, and the purchase of land for housing schemes. From the point of view of passenger transport, the most significant points concerned the planning and provision of main streets and roads in both old and new areas.

In this context Brodie posed a pertinent question: at what distance apart should main lines of communication be provided? He had been unable to discover any agreed standard, whether on the basis of population served or optimum headways, probably because tramways had normally had to follow existing roads. As far as Liverpool was concerned, the average distance apart of the tramways at the limit of the built-up area was about 800yd; the average number of houses at this point was about 25 to the acre, and the average walking distance to the nearest stop was about 500yd. He urged that if planning was to be effective, careful examination would have to be given to such criteria.

This was directly relevant to the situation in the south-east of Liverpool, where a large area between the existing built-up area and the municipal boundary was being planned. Tramways were already in operation in parts of this district (such as the routes to Calderstones Park and the new line to Broad Green) but further lines would probably be required as development proceeded. The maximum distance apart would be about 1,000yd, but this would be dependent on the number of houses to the acre as well as the amount of space given to such amenities as parks and other open spaces. Where development might take place over a period as long as 40 years, there was obviously great difficulty in forecasting transport requirements, a situation which emphasised the importance of close coordination between transport and planning.

Current traffic conditions had brought a drastic change in road planning needs; ample width was now a crucial factor in the planning of all main roads. While Brodie saw 80ft as the minimum width for any important main road leading to a major central area, he put forward a standard which was to prove basic to the development of the transport system:

'Where land can be acquired on reasonable terms, as in the outskirts of a large city, the widening of the most important main thoroughfares to 120ft can be strongly recommended wherever the street authority and the tramway authority are anxious to provide the best possible accommodation for traffic, and are prepared to work together with this object in view.'

To illustrate his case Brodie was able to point to the tramway extension then under construction from Edge Lane to Broad Green and Bowring Park; this included a 120ft wide road incorporating a dual carriageway with the tracks on a central strip:

'The tramways are laid on wooden cross sleepers on a clinker foundation, the clinker being brought up to the level of the top of the sleepers, and over this soil is laid for grass, the top of the soil being left at the level of the bottom of the head of the rail.'

So impressive was the result compared with the normal street tramway that *Tramway and Railway World* was inspired to wax almost lyrical in its description: 'In planning the extension of the Edge Lane tramway to the Bowring Estate at Roby, the Liverpool Corporation have shown a resourcefulness and adaptability which provide a fine object lesson for future tramway builders and town planners.'

The route along Edge Lane as far as South Bank Road had been opened in 1912 as the first part of a line authorised in 1909 to tap the Bowring Estate, an area of woodland with gardens and a golf course which had come into the possession of the Corporation in 1906. Further sections amounting to nearly three miles were constructed and the route was opened as far as Broad Green station in 1914, followed by completion to Bowring Park in 1915.

The new line began as normal street track, and the original proposals had envisaged an 80ft road; however, since it had been possible to purchase cheaply a strip of land alongside the road for a distance of nearly two miles, the outer sections were mostly laid as 'grass tracks', either in the centre of the carriageway or on a roadside strip, while the terminus was situated just off the road and within the park itself. The line was planned to preserve the rural aspect of the road, and *Tramway and Railway World* commended the 'trim grass plots, neat privet hedges and tree-planted footpaths' which graced the route. The outer end was actually beyond the municipal 'frontier' and was bordered by cornfields and parkland, but the district was fast developing as a residential area, with new housing in the Liverpool Garden Suburb near Broad Green. Not only were transport facilities built-in, but the welfare of local residents was reflected in

Top right: Grass-sown, tree-lined and hedged, many miles of the new style tramways were to follow the example of the Bowring Park line; extension into newly-developing areas enabled tramway and housing to be integrated. In this view of about 1915 No 196 is inbound from Bowring Park.   *H. G. Dibdin*

Centre right: A glimpse of the old Liverpool: by the 1930s population was moving out from overcrowded districts to the new suburbs. Here 'Cabin' car No 807 on its way to Old Swan negotiates the single track and loop, a layout obviously unsuited to the age of increasing motor traffic. Though much redevelopment was taking place, the high cost of land in inner areas made the extension of 'grass tracks' into the city prohibitively expensive.   *R. Brook*

Below: The spacious arrangement of the reserved-track tramways among suburban housing is exemplified by this scene on the Garston route with 'streamliner' No 932. Several miles of new tramways were laid to serve new estates in the Allerton area.   *C. Carter*

the cheap fare of only 3d (just over 1p) for the six miles from Pier Head.

From the Tramways Department's point of view, these 'grass tracks' offered two crucial advantages: lower cost and higher speed. For the 120ft road, Brodie had pointed out, the cost of building the tramway, plus the additional street widenings, was no greater than for a street 80ft wide with the usual paved tramway. In Liverpool the cost of construction of a normal street tramway (excluding the overhead equipment) was about £6,000 per mile of single line, while for a 'grass track' the equivalent figure was only about half this, at £3,000. In addition the cost of maintenance was considerably lower, since the open tracks were readily accessible without the expense of digging up and then relaying the paving, while — unlike the street track — there was no paving to be kept in order under the battering of other road traffic. Moreover, the street tramway which had to share its roadway with other traffic could not be worked at high speed, whereas the tracks on their own reservations enabled higher speeds to be attained in safety; in view of the enclosed nature of the tracks, the Board of Trade had sanctioned a speed of 20mph along the route.

For new construction into districts where land was relatively cheap, such integrated layouts were a practicable proposition; but what about the built-up areas? To prove really effective in providing fast congestion-free traffic flow, these wide roads with their reserved-track tramways needed to be continued into the central areas of the city. What then would be the cost? Brodie distinguished four types of areas and estimated the costs in each, as follows:

|  | 40ft road widened to 80ft with paved tramway (per mile) | 40ft road widened to 120ft with 'grass track' tramway (per mile) |
| --- | --- | --- |
| Undeveloped area | £29,000 | £26,000 |
| Partly built-up area | £53,000 | £65,000 |
| Built-up area needing redevelopment | £147,000 | £252,000 |
| Central area | £616,000 | £1,190,000 |

These figures showed clearly the enormous cost of extending these fine boulevards into the city centre; obviously the price-tag on central area work put it completely out of the question. It was all very well laying out these grass tracks in new suburbs, but pushing them through into the heart of the city was another matter altogether, and this was to prove a basic weakness of an extended tramway system; many miles of reserved tracks were to be constructed in the

suburbs over the next 25 years to form the infra-structure for a potential rapid transit service, but the crowded street tracks of the central areas remained to entangle the tramcars into the congealed mass of urban congestion.

Brodie was aware of the problem and spelled it out quite clearly: 'tramway traffics are likely to suffer severely in the future from the neglect of road widenings in the larger towns'. While considerable expenditure would be needed if faster services were to be provided in the city, it was worth looking at this from the point of view of obtaining the best value for money. In spite of the obstacles, he remained convinced that there was 'a fine opening in many places for an improved tramway system, if designed and carried out on lines calculated to meet effectively the other forms of conveyance at present successfully competing with existing tramways'.

To this end he believed that speed was a prime factor in the continued success of the tramway. If it had to continue to run along congested streets, where it could not show any advantage in speed, the ordinary tramway was likely to decline. 'Increased speed has come to stay, and both the town planning and tramway authorities must be prepared to provide arrangements which will meet the new conditions of life in large towns'. Average speed should be raised to around 20mph, based on an average of six stops a mile, with safe operation ensured by fenced-in reserved tracks. In his advocacy of speed Brodie was no doubt envisaging the continuing extension of tramway routes into new suburbs in outlying districts; higher speeds were called for if journey times on longer routes were not to become unattractively prolonged.

Speeds of 15-25mph were already being offered by segregated electric railways, though in this case passengers could suffer considerable loss of time because of the location of the stations, the longer distances between stations, and the less frequent services compared with an urban tramway. Nevertheless, in districts served by electric railway passengers were already leaving the local tramways; now, instead of living two or three miles from the city centre and travelling by tram, they could travel three times that distance in the same time by electric railway, and so live further out in pleasanter surroundings. Brodie already had in mind the effects of the Lancashire & Yorkshire's electric trains; the L&YR itself was looking to its own sphere of influence covering areas further from the centre, as Aspinall had enunciated.

For the tramway to maintain its own position, then, it had to be improved — not only in speed, but also in the matter of cars and track. Noise and vibration had to be reduced and comfort increased, and Brodie believed that too little attention had been paid to these factors. He was surprised, for example, that 'the application of the indiarubber or other resilient and silent tyre to tramway vehicles' had not been seriously examined in the interests of reducing the noise that seemed to be inseparable from the tramcar.

Weight reduction was another matter that called for attention, with the aim of reducing current consumption and lessening wear on tracks. The motor bus had already shown that a weight of 2cwt per passenger was practicable, compared with the 3.5cwt per passenger for the typical tramcar (though of course the motor bus had to be built to conform to severe weight restrictions and enjoyed a relatively short life, while the traditional tramcar was a sturdily constructed vehicle intended to last almost indefinitely). Again, this point seems not to have been quickly taken; the new Liverpool standard car of the 1920s had a weight per passenger of 3.8cwt.

In putting forward his parameters for the successful development of tramways in relation to town planning, Brodie had made crucial assumptions 'that those responsible for tramways will take full advantage of every development both in materials and methods, and that there will not be too great reluctance to move with the times'. The next 25 years of the Liverpool tramways proved the relevance of these assumptions, while the soundness of the principles he advocated remains no less apparent even today.

High speed operation featured in further schemes advocated by Brodie and adopted in 1921, as part of the city's suburban planning. These schemes included the reconstruction of the tramway along Princes Road, to be linked to further extensions to serve the growing districts of Woolton, Allerton and Garston, where new housing was being undertaken on a large scale in hitherto largely undeveloped areas stretching to the city boundaries. A basic part of the scheme was the extension of the fast tracks as far into the central area as possible, and to this end Princes Road was selected for widening, with the relocation of the tramway on segregated sleeper track. In conjunction with this move, the Croxteth Road route was to be projected along a widened Ullet Road to join the existing tramway on Smithdown Road, since the widening of Smithdown Road was considered to be too costly. By this means a fast entry and exit would be provided for proposed new suburban routes.

By 1924, from the existing Calderstone Park line in Menlove Avenue, new roads complete with central reservation were laid out across the housing estates: along an extended Menlove Avenue to Woolton, and into the Allerton estates on a new road (Mather Avenue) which finally reached Garston to join the Aigburth route. Expenditure on these roads and their associated tramways amounted to more than £350,000. Meanwhile part of Aigburth Road to Garston had been undergoing transformation, as

about a mile and a half of tramway in the Aigburth Vale district was rebuilt on reserved sleeper track as the road was widened.

One missing link in the transport pattern was the absence of the proposed Ullet Road line; Woolton and Allerton services were constrained by having to use the more congested Smithdown Road to get into the city instead of the Princes Road sleeper track, which served only to speed the Aigburth and Garston services. This lack emphasised the weakness resulting from the absence of fast tracks within the central districts, in which Princes Road would have been a prototype; the omission was increasingly felt as motor traffic multiplied over the coming years, to the detriment of regular public transport operation.

Meanwhile more tramways were being built in the new north-eastern suburbs. The focus of these was the vast Norris Green estate, the most ambitious of the city's housing developments where homes by the thousand were erected during the 1920s and 1930s on land only recently brought within the municipal boundary. Through the rows of council dwellings marched broad thoroughfares dignified as 'avenues' — Utting Avenue, Townsend Avenue, Muirhead Avenue — with a few 'lanes' thrown in for good measure to recall the rural character rapidly disappearing under the bricks and mortar — Lower Lane, Dwerryhouse Lane. And along these avenues and lanes ran the grass-track tramways to create one of Britain's most ambitious integrated transport and housing schemes. Tramways were laid on sleeper tracks along these suburban roads; into the new estates on the north-east of the city, along Muirhead Avenue in 1923, Utting Avenue and Townsend Avenue in 1924, along Walton Hall Avenue to the start of the East Lancashire Road at Stopgate Lane in 1925. To the south-east the tracks were laid along the outer part of Menlove Avenue to Woolton and along Mather Avenue to Allerton. Further extensions in the north-east came during the 1930s: Townsend Avenue and Utting Avenue again in 1937, and further along the East Lancashire Road to Lower Lane the following year, then onward to Stonebridge Lane and Gillmoss in 1940-41.

While most of the country's cities and towns witnessed the inevitable march of suburbia during this period, Liverpool's basically tram-orientated estates demonstrated a coordination of transport and planning to meet dual aims; first, the use of the most economic and efficient mode of transport under the conditions in which it could serve most advantageously; this meant the existing tramways which had proved their economy and which — based on the principles already enumerated by the city's Engineer — could be built-in to an effective road system at reasonable cost to provide speedy and efficient services; and, secondly, the provision of transport services at the lowest

Above: The setting of a typical stopping place on the reserved-track tramways, complete with waiting shelter, is well shown in this view of No 284 on the Page Moss service. *R. Brook*

Right: 'Green Goddess' streamliners at Longview Lane on the roadside reserved track of the Prescot route. Considerable expenditure was incurred by both Liverpool Corporation and the County Council in the reconstruction of the interurban Prescot tramway during the 1920s. *R. Brook*

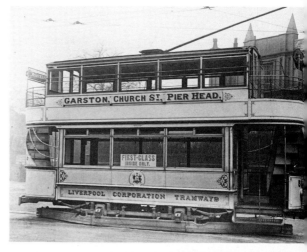

Top right: Class distinction: sparklingly new in 1908, Liverpool Corporation first class tramcar No 506 poses at Dingle in the full glory of its white livery, elaborate lining and elegantly lettered destination boards. An extra charge was made for riding in the first class cars, which continued until 1923, enabling the respectable middle classes to travel safely segregated from the lower orders. *H. G. Dibdin*

Centre right: The role of Liverpool's early motor buses: with solid tyres and open top deck, Corporation AEC KB1981 works an outer suburban route between Garston and Woolton. *N. N. Forbes*

Below: Tramcars for all. Whitechapel crossing in 1908; top-covered standard car No 225 halts while another car of the same type passes on the cross-city Aintree-Aigburth service. Note the painters at work on the overhead standards in the foreground; the profusion of ironwork required constant attention against the ravages of corrosion in salt-laden sea air, while at the same time tramway operators had to pay rates on fixed equipment and maintain road surfaces. *H. G. Dibdin*

possible cost for the benefit of the new suburban residents. The city's housing estates were intended as a vast removal project; their object was to take the pressure off the notoriously overcrowded inner areas of the city. Many of the new suburbanites came from homes demolished under slum clearance plans; now resettled often far from their place of work, they depended upon cheap transport.

Instead of living within a two to three-mile radius or the city centre or the docks, they now lived five or six miles away; hence journeys to and from work were longer and fares were higher. Social justice dictated that transport services should be as cheap and as speedy as possible if such people were not to be seriously disadvantaged. 'We have to carry the people there at a very small charge', Councillor A. Morrow, a member of the Transport Committee, pointed out. 'We have developed housing estates at such distances from the city that the people cannot afford high fares to go there, and we have to cater for them accordingly.' As far as Liverpool was concerned, this meant a maximum fare of 2d on the tramcar.

## A Place for the Bus

*Is there anybody outside a Tramway Committee who would carry two people, their luggage and their children some 8 miles for 4d the lot?*
Alderman F. Smith, Vice Chairman, Liverpool Corporation Tramways Committee, 1926

In 1907 Liverpool's Tramways Committee, reporting to the City Council on 'the suggested installation of a service of motor omnibuses', concluded that 'the time has not yet arrived when this class of vehicle could be operated in the city with any hope of financial success'. Four years later, however, the Corporation went into the motor bus business with the takeover of Woolton and District Motor Services, and in the next two years Tilling-Stevens petrol-electric buses were in operation and the Tramways Committee was ordering three different types of motor buses to determine which would prove most suitable for its purposes. By 1914 three routes were running. One was in effect an extension of the tramway from the Calderstones Park terminus to the outlying village of Woolton; the second was a cross-suburban link between Aigburth and Old Swan; and the third filled in a gap between tram routes from Seaforth to Walton. During the course of that year about a million passengers were carried on the buses, a tiny figure compared with more than 140 million on the Corporation's tramcars, but nevertheless a significant indication that the trams were not to have things all their own way.

Another role seemed to be opening for the motor

bus after World War 1; the Tramways Committee authorised a scheme for the introduction of a hundred buses to 'assist' the tramways, which were proving unable to cope with the increasing demand. The trams in 1918 were carrying nearly 50 million passengers more than in 1914, but it was impossible to obtain new cars to augment the existing fleet which was suffering from the effects of wartime overwork and under-maintenance. Under the proposal, the buses would as far as possible keep away from the main streets served by the tramcars, in order to minimise the congestion that might result if both forms of transport followed the same streets, though such a separation might be thought to nullify something of the 'assistance' value of the buses.

An intriguing aspect of the scheme was the running of buses 'at high speed' on certain sections of their journeys, so that they could offer an 'express' service that would be faster than the trams, an interesting anticipation of the limited-stop bus concept which highlighted a major inflexibility of the large tramway system in that fast and slow cars could not run together over the same tracks.

But Liverpool's trams were not to be so easily defeated. The rail-favoured policy was reiterated: buses would not be permitted to compete with the tramway services, but would be allowed to act as no more than 'a most desirable adjunct'. And to reinforce the point in practical terms the city decreed the provision of an additional 100 tramcars. The decision was backed by sound economics; as the Tramways Manager pointed out, Liverpool's experience was that tramways paid, while buses did not: 'Per passenger mile the tramcar costs much less than the omnibus.'

The reasons were not far to seek; the low capacity of the bus made it impossible to operate at a profit with fares at the low level charged on the trams, while the disadvantage was compounded by the fact that the buses were confined to the less busy routes where they might spend much of their time running with loads well below capacity. There was an answer, as *Tramway and Railway World* pointed out:
'No discouragement should be felt by Liverpool Tramways Committee at the loss of £5,000 on their omnibuses during the past year... The remedy is indicated by the Committee who state that omnibuses with the present seating capacity cannot be operated remuneratively on the present fares. Steps should therefore be taken as soon as possible to increase the charges...'

While such a move might have made sound economic sense, it was not considered socially equitable; what justification could there be for charging some citizens higher fares than others? The basis of a municipal service had to be fair treatment for all.

A comparison of the contemporary tram and bus gives us an interesting insight into the respective attractions of each. The standard tramcar was a double-deck four-wheeler mounted on a Brill truck of 7ft 6in wheelbase and powered by two 40hp motors. Though the upper deck was covered in, the balconies and platforms were unenclosed. Seats 'constructed entirely of maple' were provided for 22 passengers on the lower deck and for 38 on the upper. Bodywork was built of 'well seasoned English oak, reinforced by substantial wrought-iron plates, floorings and roof of pitch pine, with waist rails of teak, and mahogany panels'.

Representing the bus fleet of the time was an AEC double-decker with the advanced feature of an enclosed top deck. Although the lower deck was built of the traditional wood, the upper deck was constructed largely of duralumin, a metal alloy lighter than wood and developed for use in airships. Weight restrictions imposed on road vehicles dictated the adoption of such lightweight materials, while no comparable limitations applied to the tramcar, no doubt an important factor in maintaining its conventional bulky build. Although the tram's solid wood construction enabled it to enjoy an almost indefinite working life, the greater deadweight it was obliged to carry around over the years must have been reflected in its speed and current consumption. Meanwhile our specimen bus, powered by a 45hp petrol engine, provided seating for a total of 55 passengers, much more than most buses and only five fewer than the tram, and a reminder that the motor bus was developing into a serious rival. Of this total, 26 were carried on the lower deck, and 27 on the long knifeboard seats on the upper deck; a reminder of a different age in road transport is the fact that two additional passengers could be seated in the driver's cab, a much coveted position for the enthusiast. And this cab really was a cab; it had a windscreen and a seat for the driver, while the unfortunate tram motormen had to stand on an open platform.

A report presented in 1926 by the Tramways Manager Percy Priestly still put the motor bus firmly in its place as a subsidiary to the tramways:
'While the omnibus is a useful vehicle as a feeder to the tramway system and for running upon routes where the traffic is not such as to warrant the expenditure required for laying a tramway permanent way, it cannot in any way compete with the tramcar for dealing with the enormous number of people travelling during the traffic peak loads.'

Because of the smaller capacity of the bus, he pointed out, the 580 tramcars needed in peak-hour service would require to be replaced by nearly 900 buses, thus increasing the number of vehicles by about 50%.

Priestly went on to examine suggestions that the tramways should be scrapped, and his arguments are clearly indicative of the weight of vested interest which, in Liverpool as in many other cities and towns, served to sustain the life of the tramways even after the motor bus had become a practicable alternative. Liverpool's tramway undertaking represented a capital investment of almost £3 million; if it were to be scrapped, charges on interest and sinking fund would have to be borne from the bus revenue. Considerable expenditure would have to be incurred in obtaining the necessary number of buses; moreover these would have a life of only about 7 to 10 years, compared with 15 to 20 years for the tram. Further, the tramways were closely allied to other sectors of the municipal economy; they paid about £45,000 a year in rates, as well as around £50,000 a year on road maintenance; if the trams were not there to bear such burdens, these sums would have to be met out of the general rate, and would amount to the equivalent of a 4d rate.

Yet the tramways were still able to absorb these extraneous impositions and come up smiling; not only did they turn in a profit, but they could provide cheaper fares than the buses: they could offer fares averaging only 0.5d per mile, while the buses could not survive on less than about 0.75d. Operating statistics revealed the trams in a very healthy state; receipts per car mile were more than 20d, while total operating expenses were only 16d, so leaving a comfortable surplus of 4d for every mile run by each car. No wonder your penny fare entitled you to a two-mile ride. Economies of scale were effective in the large Liverpool undertaking; by contrast, for a penny fare in Wallasey you could travel just over a mile, and in Birkenhead less than three-quarters of a mile. It seemed to be a case of 'big is better'.

Priestly returned to the tram-versus-bus question in a further report to the City Council in 1929, when he reached a similar conclusion. 'Under present conditions the motor omnibus could not compete with the tramcar in dealing with the rush-hour traffic, nor in giving cheap fares for long-distance travelling'. To carry the city's peak traffic, the services of 640 trams were required, and because of the lower carrying capacity of the bus, these would have to be replaced by no fewer than 880 buses, representing almost a 40% increase in the number of vehicles. Obviously such a change would mean a substantial rise in running costs as well as an addition to the congestion of crowded city streets.

Surprisingly, there was little difference in operating cost per vehicle mile; but in view of the difference in capacity, the cost per seat mile for the bus was still more than 50% greater than for the tramcar. It would therefore have been economically impracticable for the buses to charge the low fares which were offered on

Above: Still dominant, the tramcars had occasion to celebrate; here Liverpool Corporation No 544 stands outside Green Lane depot specially decorated on the occasion of a royal visit to the city in 1913. *H. G. Dibdin*

Below: The motor bus grows up; tall and dignified, Birkenhead Corporation Motor's No 31 was one of eight Leyland Leviathans acquired in 1925 to replace tramcars. It had a 52-seat Leyland body, though it is unofficially reported that as many as 100 passengers might be crammed aboard on the Moreton route on an August holiday. The oil-lamp pattern headlights add a touch of old-world elegance. *Ian Allan Library*

the trams; their fares would have to be some 50% higher.

Figures were again quoted to indicate the extent of the financial commitment. The tramway undertaking now represented a capital investment of almost £3½ million, with the amount outstanding coming to more than £1¼ million. If the tramways were scrapped, payments for interest and sinking fund would have to be met from bus revenue, which would also have to cover the cost (an estimated further £250,000) of reinstating the roadway after the tracks were lifted. Added to this would be a capital expenditure of some £1¾ million on new buses to replace the existing tramcar fleet. Again, therefore, the tramways were revealed as a massive vested interest, their very existence tending towards their self-perpetuation.

Nor could they be considered in isolation; more figures were adduced to substantiate their place in the municipal economy. The tramways continued to pay to the city's treasury more than £50,000 a year in rates in respect of their tracks in the streets. In addition they had to spend about £40,000 a year on road maintenance under the provisions of the 1870 Tramways Act which required the undertaking to maintain the road surface between and on each side of the tracks; over the previous 10 years Liverpool's Tramways Department had incurred expenditure under this heading of more than £1 million. So if the tramways were abolished, not only would the city lose a substantial ratepayer, but this road expenditure would fall on the general rate. The tramways also formed one of the largest customers for the city's electricity department, paying a bill of more than £200,000 a year for the current they consumed. From the earliest days electric tramways had been envisaged as a major load to the municipal electricity undertaking, and the loss of such a load would obviously upset the calculations. As an added bonus, the electricity department was enjoying the free use of the overhead standards for carrying its street lights.

Abolition of the tramways would therefore have had ramifications through other sectors of the municipal economy, including the treasury, the highways department and the electricity department. Taken all round, there was a strong case for leaving well alone, and indeed such an argument aided in prolonging the life of tramways in some places where strict economic principles might have dictated a more ruthless approach. As far as Liverpool was concerned, Priestly concluded that replacement by motor buses 'would not be a sound or an economical proposition'.

In certain circumstances, nevertheless, the motor bus could not be gainsaid, and Priestly now identified four types of services for which the bus was the most suitable mode of transport. First, there were services in the more thinly populated areas where the amount of traffic offering was not sufficient to justify the high cost of track construction. Second, there were services which acted as 'feeders', bringing passengers from outlying districts to the nearest tram route, where they were obliged to change vehicles to complete their journeys. Third, somewhat similar services connected the outer termini, to provide circumferential routes which obviated the need for cross-suburban passengers to travel into the city and out again. Finally, some services connected adjacent industrial districts, perhaps running only at peak hours to cater for factory workers. Taken together, all these categories amounted to little more than a subsidiary, and generally unremunerative, role for the bus.

The strength of the case for the tramcar may be judged from a look at a few figures covering operations in the year 1930. At this time the fleet totalled about 750 cars, and although the bus fleet had grown to about 180, they were carrying only about 24 million passengers in the year against nearly 260 million carried by the trams. Operating expenses per vehicle mile were still not so very different between the two modes; the bus cost slightly more at something over 15d, against a little over 14½d for the tram. But the great difference was in the revenue per vehicle mile; the tramcar earned nearly 17d while its rival brought in little more than 13d. The bus was therefore operating at a loss; on average it lost 2d for every mile it ran. And this was in spite of a higher fare scale; the average distance you could travel on the bus for 1d was just under 1¼ mile, compared with two miles on the tram. The key to its unprofitability was indicated by the fact that its average load was only 7½ passengers per mile, while the tram averaged 13 passengers per mile; this of course reflected the more restricted role of the bus in serving the less heavily-trafficked routes.

Total income of the trams for the year amounted to £1,405,000 while their total operating expenses came to £1,216,000, leaving a healthy gross profit of £189,000. For the buses, income was only £178,000 while expenses totalled £205,000, so that they ended up showing a deficit of £27,000. The situation was summed up in the operating ratio: the percentage of operating expenses to receipts in the case of the trams was 86.5%, while for the buses it was 115%. There could be no doubt which was the more profitable mode of transport in the city.

The position of the tramways in the municipal economy was long a subject of debate; how far should they make a profit, and how far should any profits be ploughed back into the undertaking to reduce fares rather than handed over to relieve the rates? An insight into the view held in Liverpool is given us by comments made in the late 1920s by Alderman F. Smith, Vice Chairman of the city's Tramways Committee. 'I wish every tramway manager and every

Top left: Lack of capacity could hardly have been a problem with this massive six-wheel Karrier with Corporation-built body of the late 1920s, but operating factors long made Liverpool's motor bus services an uneconomic part of municipal activities. KA3192, seen here on the way to Aigburth, is working a suburban route along the orbital Queens Drive. *N. N. Forbes*

Centre left: Tramcars remained the profitable mode of transport in the city, with the great bulk of traffic consisting of penny fares on short densely-loaded routes. At Old Swan in 1920, cars 213 and 162 stand ready to return to the city by their respective ways. *H. G. Dibdin*

Below: The elegant lines of Liverpool Corporation's single-deck bus fleet of the late 1920s and early 1930s are well depicted in this view of one of the Thornycrofts with the Corporation's design of clerestory-roof body. Some vehicles wore a dignified livery of grey for a time. *N. N. Forbes*

tramway committee man would look at the subject as if he were effectively running it as a private business', he told the Municipal Tramways Association's conference in 1927. 'He, as proprietor, would be entitled to a livelihood out of it, or else he could not keep his job going. And if the proprietor is entitled to a livelihood, surely the ratepayers, who find the money, are entitled to something?'

Alderman Smith returned to this theme at the following year's conference. Referring to the rating of municipal tramways, he said: 'In my view, we ought to contribute to the rates. I know some people think we ought not do so, but after all we are appointed by the ratepayers to look after their interests. We are their servants and not their masters, and if we say to them that they should not get the fruits of the labours of their representatives, then we ought to get the sack!' By contrast to this commercial approach, Alderman Smith also urged the social value of low fares. He believed that fares should be fixed at such a level that 'even the most poorly paid cannot afford to walk'. Mass travel at minimum fare had long been the basis of success for the electric tramway, as he went on to imply: 'I would make the tramways pay in this way: that it would not pay any man in employment to walk, because of the saving in time and the saving in energy.'

The city indeed prided itself on the low level of its fares. A report by the Tramways Committee in 1931 concluded that the introduction of special workmen's fares was not justified, since Liverpool's ordinary fares were as low as workmen's fares in most other cities; in fact, the Committee found only 13 places where workmen's fares were cheaper than Liverpool's ordinary fares. And nowhere else could passengers travel as far for the penny fare as the two miles offered in Liverpool.

Such bargain travel was confirmed in the following year in a report by Priestly who, after examining 60 different undertakings, calculated that their penny fare gave an average ride of only 1,622yd as compared with Liverpool's 2 miles 150yd. For the 2d fare the average distance was 2 miles 292yd, while Liverpool's 2d fare gave 4 miles 1,061yd. The average fare per mile on the 60 undertakings was 0.92d, which was more than double Liverpool's 0.44d.

By the middle of the 1920s the municipal tram was under attack from the motor bus, especially that of the private operator who could in many cases enter the business without restriction or formality and then proceed to take traffic away from established undertakings. Municipal tramways were an obvious target with their busy urban routes, and in his presidential address to the Municipal Tramways Association in 1926 Priestly raised the question of protection. 'The time is swiftly approaching', he declared, 'when it must be determined whether local authorities shall or shall not be dominant in the realm of road passenger transport service'. Should the established tramway systems be protected, in view of the rising costs of road maintenance and the proliferation of the motor bus, or should they be regarded as obsolete and be replaced by some better and cheaper means of transport?

Priestly was in no doubt of the answer. 'Tramways are unsurpassed for the cheap conveyance of great masses of the population in industrial areas, and they have proved that no other vehicle yet placed upon the road can deal with the peak load traffic in our great cities and industrial areas as economically and efficiently as they do'. Tramways had to provide services at all times of the day, issue workmen's tickets at reduced fares, pay for the cost of road maintenance, and pay rates. If bus undertakings were encumbered with the same burdens, 'it would be impossible for them to give the excellent services now provided by tramways at the present cheap scale of fares'. Moreover, because of the smaller carrying capacity of the bus, a larger number of vehicles would be required, so that street congestion would be increased.

While tramways were not afraid of fair competition, he went on, it was unreasonable that they should have to bear unfair burdens, which at the same time relieved the competing buses of what should rightly have been their responsibility. He believed that local authorities which already operated tramways should be given powers to run motor buses or trolleybuses to connect their tramway routes and to serve as feeders to them. Further, they should be permitted to join up with the systems of neighbouring local authorities to provide through services. The time for coordination was obviously imminent.

## Tramcars and Congestion

*Tramcar services carry the vast majority of the people using the streets, and . . . such services are entitled to prior consideration over other general road users.*

W. G. Marks, General Manager, Liverpool Corporation Transport Department, 1936

In 1913 Liverpool City Council passed a public-spirited if somewhat optimistic resolution:
'That it be an instruction to the Tramways and Electric Power and Lighting Committee to forthwith set about providing more cars with a view to reducing the overcrowding there now is at certain times, and the securing for all passengers what their fares entitle them to: that is, a seat from the commencement to the end of their journey.'

In his subsequent report, the Tramways Manager C. W. Mallins made it clear that the Council's aim was unattainable, a view that would be echoed by

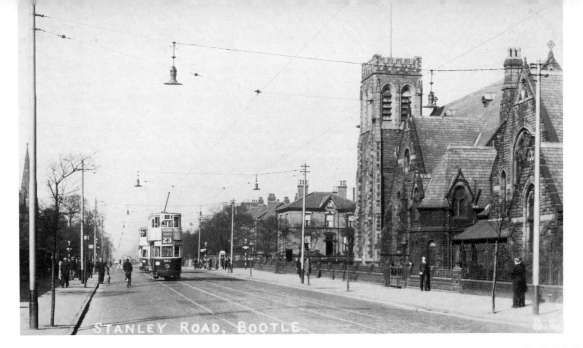
STANLEY ROAD, BOOTLE.

Above: A pleasant view along Stanley Road, Bootle, with Liverpool tramcars bound for Seaforth. Apart from the occasional cyclist, the trams still have the road very much to themselves in this scene from about 1930. *H. G. Dibdin*

Centre right: One of Liverpool's main traffic arteries, Smithdown Road by the middle of the 1930s was showing symptoms of the rising tide of motor vehicles, and the high-speed operation of suburban tramcar services posed a problem. Approaching is No 365, a standard car fitted with top cover but otherwise apparently innocent of concessions to modernity. *H. G. Dibdin*

Bottom right: Motor traffic is already a problem in central districts even in the early 1930s when this picture was taken in Church Street. Although tramcars still dominate the carriageway, streams of private cars and buses are contending for position. In the centre, traffic signals are in action, but some people (including Transport Manager Marks) doubted their efficiency in speeding the traffic flow. *H. G. Dibdin*

SMITHDOWN ROAD, LIVERPOOL.

transport managers to the present day. The problem was not peculiar to Liverpool; it was encountered by practically every tramway undertaking (and he had contacted 72 of them in the course of his investigations), and in spite of their efforts 'up to the present it has been found quite impossible to obviate the difficulty'. It seemed to be a fact of urban life, engendered by the coming of electric traction; cheap and fast transport enabled 'the working masses' to travel to and from their work, but this travelling was inevitably confined to a few hours in the day.

Two factors needed to be considered: the convenience of the travelling public and the financial implications. To eliminate overcrowding by banning standing in the cars during the peak periods would obviously cause inconvenience to many; in any case, standing was not necessarily regarded by the passenger as a great hardship, since (as in Liverpool with its preponderance of short-distance travel) the average time spent standing on the journey was only about 10 minutes.

The provision of enough cars to enable every passenger to travel seated would entail considerable extra expenditure, which would not be covered by any gain in revenue. Mallins reckoned that 120 extra cars would be required; these would be used for only about $3\frac{1}{2}$ hours each day, but the additional annual expenditure would amount to some £57,000. The best method of minimising the problem would be to introduce cars with larger seating capacity; a new type of car was already in the experimental stage, but clearly this was a longer term project.

Reinforcing his argument, Mallins went on to point to the congested nature of the central area of the city, where traffic had almost reached the limits of capacity and where it would have been impracticable to have run additional cars with any degree of regularity. As it was, tramway services were subject to considerable delay during busy periods, resulting in irregular running which was the cause of many complaints. 'The headway available in the centre of the city is so small', he said, 'that the cars can only move at a slow pace, resulting in a considerable loss in the use of the cars, and in consumption of current and serious injury to the electrical equipment, apart from the loss of time to the travelling public'.

One method of trying to alleviate congestion had been proved a failure. New tracks had been constructed so as to enable Lime Street and Old Haymarket to become the termini for some of the cars, which would therefore not have to traverse such congested thoroughfares as Church Street, Lord Street, Dale Street or Water Street. However, passenger flows were such that services needed to run into the central area and to the Pier Head, and the short-working cars had been poorly patronised. The obvious lesson was

that public transport had to meet public demand; cutting it short on the edge of the central area was no real answer to the problem (though it was to be recommended more than once in later years).

In view of the congestion and the increasing amount of traffic to and from the city centre and the landing stage, Mallins urged the construction of a third tramway route to the Mersey. Two were already in existence: by way of Church Street, Lord Street and James Street, and through Dale Street and Water Street. He suggested that a third route could be provided by the widening of some streets. A more revolutionary proposal was for a subway, which could be built from Old Haymarket to the Pier Head, with 'stations' at suitable places en route; this would not only relieve the existing tracks, but would create an unobstructed route capable of handling any foreseeable increase in passenger traffic in the future. Either scheme would of course be costly, but 'the traffic congestion problem is becoming so urgent that the solution cannot much longer be delayed'.

In his report to the City Council in 1929, Mallins' successor Percy Priestly disputed the assertion that the trams were a major cause of congestion, a growing matter for concern in a period when the motor vehicle was multiplying rapidly. On the contrary, Priestly claimed, the fact that they followed a fixed path along the streets served to divert other vehicles to either side of the tracks and so helped to regulate the flow of traffic. As to the advantage asserted for the bus that it was able to pull in to the kerb to pick up and set down its passengers, he thought it likely that such weaving movements would only intensify rush-hour delays in the city's crowded thoroughfares like Lord Street, Church Street and Dale Street. 'Congestion and delays in the streets are not due to the running of tramways,' he stated firmly; tramcars could accelerate faster than buses, and they could attain just as high a speed.

The real cause of congestion, Priestly concluded, was that nearly all the city centre traffic had to be funnelled along only two main routes, Lord Street — Church Street and Dale Street. In busy city streets it probably did not make much difference whether you had trams or buses; either way, you were likely to have congestion as well. By contrast, in the suburbs the tramcars had the advantage of a substantial mileage of 'grass tracks', along which the Ministry of Transport had sanctioned a higher speed (20mph) than on any other tramway undertaking in Britain. Once clear of the central area, therefore, they were able to convey their passengers to outlying suburbs within a reasonable time. And not only were trams safer (their braking efficiency was greater than on any other road vehicle) but they could keep going in foggy weather when other traffic had been brought to a halt.

Further vindication of the city's tramways was

Top left: Traffic to and from the docks traditionally formed a distinctive part of Liverpool's transport pattern; in this animated scene in Pall Mall about 1920, most of the haulage work is still done by horses, though one motor truck returning empty is prominent on the left, its speed governed by that of the horse wagons. *Merseyside PTE*

Centre left: The city's traffic problems epitomised: an illustration from Liverpool Transport Manager Marks' report of 1936 shows how parked cars reduce the effective width of the street, forcing slow-moving horse-drawn wagons on to the tram tracks and so delaying tramcars and other traffic. There is even a hand-cart (far left) to add to the confusion. The location is Renelagh Street. *Merseyside PTE*

Below: Illustrations from W. G. Marks' 1936 report depict Liverpool's congestion problem. Not only was motor traffic increasing, but parked cars added to congestion in busy streets, as here in Dale Steet (left) where the flow of tramcars is hindered and a regular service rendered impossible. 'Public service vehicles should be given every possible facility for free and easy passage along the streets of the city', Marks stressed. Meanwhile (right) tramcars wait patiently while a horse-drawn wagon crosses Dale Street; the diminution in the number of horse-drawn vehicles in the 1930s offered some compensation for the rise in the volume of motor vehicles. *Merseyside PTE*

made in the 1930 report of Sir Henry Maybury (formerly of the Roads Department of the Ministry of Transport) who had been engaged in the previous year to examine Liverpool's traffic problems. The tramways, he concluded, represented an excellent investment, 'capable of serving the public extremely well for many years and of earning large sums of money for the ratepayers'. The current financial situation was sufficient indication of the basic soundness of the undertaking. However, in detail Sir Henry was critical of the cars themselves, which he claimed had not kept pace with the demand for greater speed and comfort. Urgently needed now was a new design, capable of higher speeds and offering a better standard of comfort for the passenger. It should be a bogie vehicle capable of accommodating 70 to 74 passengers on upholstered seats; its larger capacity would enhance its effectiveness in rush-hour operations and so contribute to ameliorating the problem of congestion. The successful future of the system demanded the introduction of better cars as soon as possible, he concluded.

At the same time, Sir Henry believed it would be 'unwise' to consider any extension of the tramway system, in view of the great improvement being made in both trolleybus and motor bus. He did not think that trolleybuses would replace Liverpool's tramcars, but he suggested that it should be Corporation policy to add to the city's transport operations by the greater use of motor buses. As to an underground, he did not believe that this could prove an economic proposition, but traffic problems within Liverpool would be eased by the completion of the Mersey Tunnel, especially if the proposed Everton Tunnel was also constructed in order to provide direct access from the docks and the city centre to the new artery of the East Lancashire Road. Traffic congestion remained a perennial problem, and a further report in 1936 by Liverpool's Transport Manager W. G. Marks examined its causes and remedies again, and made out a strong case for giving priority to public transport:
'The vast majority of the inhabitants of the city and its environs depend upon the transport services provided by the Corporation, both for business and pleasure . . . and preference should be given to such services in the free use of the streets.'

Marks criticised the fact that traffic restrictions were nearly always applied to public transport rather than to private motor vehicles. He went on to make a spirited defence of the city's tramcar services:
'Much has been said and written by certain sections of the public and the press about the obstruction caused by tramcars, and many totally unjust allegations have been levelled at this form of passenger transport.'

Contending that the tramcar did not present such an obstruction as was sometimes alleged, he maintained that, because of its high carrying capacity, it was still the most efficient means of mass street transport. He adduced figures to support his argument; on an ordinary weekday about 677,000 passengers used the city's tramways. Of this total, some 332,000 (or almost 50%) travelled during the peak periods from 7 to 9am and from 4 to 8pm; and of this 332,000, about 200,000 travelled between the suburbs and the central area.

These figures immediately served to emphasise two of the transport department's problems. First, the intensity of the peak-hour load called for much capacity which was overloaded at these times but was little used outside the peaks. Second, suburban traffic was growing in importance as the new housing estates developed on the outskirts of the city.

The space-effectiveness of the tramcar was also demonstrated. A survey had shown that during one evening between 4.30 and 6.30, 304 trams had passed along Church Street in one direction, carrying a total of 14,800 passengers, an average of 48 passengers per car. During the same time, 190 private motor cars had passed, carrying a total of only about 350 passengers, an average of a mere 1.85 persons per car. Which type of transport, Marks asked, was making the best use of the city's busy streets?

Yet it was the motor vehicle that was rapidly growing in numbers. Marks quoted more figures to show the expansion in just five years: within Liverpool the number of private cars had risen from about 9,400 in 1930 to nearly 13,300 in 1935, a rise of about 40% — clearly not everyone was suffering from the economic depression! The number of goods motor vehicles over the same period had increased less dramatically but still substantially: from 5,500 to 6,400, a rise of more than 15%. On the other hand the mileage operated by the city's tramcars and buses showed only a very small increase, so they could not be the cause of the worsening congestion.

The upsurge in motor traffic was of course a national phenomenon; the motor industry was now turning out cheap cars by mass production methods. More specific to a commercial area such as Liverpool was the greater use of road transport rather than rail for goods haulage; more and more loads to and from the docks were traversing the city's streets as traders found the motor lorry a more convenient and flexible mode of transport for their products. Again specific to Liverpool, the newly opened Mersey Tunnel provided an additional means of cross-river communication, thus encouraging a greater volume of road traffic to pass through the city centre.

Short-term measures to improve the situation, Marks claimed, should include parking restrictions

Above: The plight of the pedestrian in the motor age was eased by the installation of clearly defined crossings on which they had the right of way (the 'Belisha beacon' can be seen on the left in this photograph taken in Ranelagh Street in 1936). But Marks contended that these crossings added further inconvenience to traffic flow, and 'the delays caused by them to vehicular traffic must lead to the construction of pedestrian subways'. *Merseyside PTE*

Left: 'Main streets were provided for the movement of live vehicles, not the storage of dead ones', Liverpool's Transport Manager stated in 1936 when he produced this view (above) of Dale Street to show how a line of parked vehicles forced traffic on to the tram tracks in the centre of the street. Some 20 years later, although the tramcars have gone the problem remains; (below) parked cars at the kerb in St John's Lane oblige Leyland L865 to halt in the middle of the carriageway to unload, to the inconvenience of both passengers and traffic. *Merseyside PTE*

and priority for public transport at junctions, both of which measures have a modern ring to them, so persistent are the problems. There is a modern look too about Marks' dictum: 'Main streets were provided for the movement of live vehicles, not the storage of dead ones'. He castigated the indiscriminate parking which often reduced the effective width of the city streets by 50%; this, rather than his trams, lay at the root of central congestion. He had many times noticed that one parked car in a street forced a slow-moving stream of traffic, perhaps headed by a horse-drawn dray, to occupy the tram tracks, with the result that a procession of tramcars built up behind; people waiting in the suburbs consequently complained that the trams were running in 'bunches' and dubbed them 'banana' cars. Buses fared no better; cars parked at stops forced the buses to halt in the middle of the carriageway, so delaying following traffic. Meanwhile, he noted rather acidly, the Corporation's car parks remained less than full.

'I have arrived definitely at the conclusion', Marks stated, 'that the main reason for congestion and for irregularity of services of public service vehicles operating between the city and the suburban areas is the parking of cars in the streets in the busy portions of the city.' To illustrate the effect of parked vehicles, he revealed that tramcars had been taking an average of 13 minutes in the peak to get from Pier Head to the Adelphi, but as a result of police action in tackling the problem of the parked car, this time had been reduced to less than 10 minutes, a saving of more than three minutes per tramcar. As a result of this action the regularity of services could be noticeably improved. In this case the effect of parking had been to lengthen the journey time of public transport vehicles by more than 30%.

Nor were the traffic control schemes proving entirely effective in speeding the flow. Liverpool had installed automatic traffic signals at busy junctions, not only to enhance road safety but also to reduce costs compared with the employment of the traditional point-duty policeman. Marks was not convinced that this was a good bargain; while the policeman could give priority to the busy mainstream or avoid delays by speedily giving the 'come on' once cross-traffic had cleared the junctions, the unseeing and unthinking automatic signals were completely inflexible in their operation. Consequently, delays led to bunching of services and irregular running. The early traffic signal systems, of which Liverpool was a pioneer, of course worked on a fixed-interval sequence; vehicle-actuated signals, their timing controlled by the volume of traffic on each road, were still something of a novelty.

A survey taken in the morning rush between 9 and 10 o'clock at the crossing of Lord Street with North John Street showed that of more than 350 tramcars travelling along Lord Street during this hour, nearly half were delayed because the signal lights were against them, even though no other traffic was crossing. The average delay per tramcar was almost 13 seconds; this may not have seemed much in isolation, but the aggregate time lost came to nearly 35 minutes, and this was in the course of only one hour. The consequences were obvious: not only were journey times lengthened for thousands of passengers in a hurry to get to their work, but services became irregular as cars 'bunched' into convoys.

To make matters worse, the same problem extended into the suburbs where it might have been expected that some of the lost time could have been regained. At the junction of Queens Drive and Walton Hall Avenue, for example, the automatic signals were again interposing delay; in one hour, nearly half of the 32 cars negotiating the junction were held up at the lights when no other traffic was crossing, and here the average delay was nearly 20 seconds. Although a hold-up of a few seconds may appear trivial by itself, a succession of such delays to a high proportion of the cars caused havoc to the regularity of a close-headway schedule.

A significant point about the effects of congestion on the public transport flow was the irregularity it introduced into the services. This, rather than any inadequacy of capacity, was the main cause of complaint; the passenger could never be sure of his vehicle arriving at the scheduled time. A service might have a nominal 10-minute headway, but conditions made it impossible to ensure regular intervals between vehicles; 'bunching', coupled with long barren periods of impatient waiting, aroused the ire of passengers anxious to get to work or to return home after their toils. To this, no effective answer has yet been found.

In Liverpool an added complication was the splitting of services in the central area. Trams bound for Broad Green and Bowring Park, for example, travelled alternately via Church Street and Dale Street, with a 12-minute headway on each route so as to give a combined six-minute frequency over the main part of the route. However, this offered two hostages to fortune; holdups in either Church Street or Dale Street effectively disrupted the neat pattern of regularity. Marks recommended an end to such split operations; all vehicles on one service should be sent along the same streets. By this means they could all suffer equally while, in theory at least, the equal headway should be more or less maintained. Although some passengers would be at a disadvantage by the withdrawal of one service, this would be compensated by improved frequency and regularity on the other. 'Public passenger vehicles should have priority at junctions when ready to cross, and this the automatic signal is unable to give.' Marks suggested that police

Below: Tramcars were often blamed for causing congestion in Liverpool's central streets, but the density of traffic along a limited number of main thoroughfares made delays inevitable. At the same time it was accepted that new and faster tramcars were needed to accelerate the services; in this scene in Derby Square in the early 1930s No 557, one of the many Bellamy-type cars built between 1907 and 1912, still features open platforms and balconies, as well as reversed stairs; it contrasts with one of the later all-enclosed standard cars seen on the right. *R. Brook*

Bottom : Even into the 1930s Corporation buses were not too abundant in most central streets of Liverpool; here one of the characteristic Thornycrofts with Corporation-built body passes St George's Hall. The line of motor vehicles on the right recalls the part attributed to the parked car in adding to congestion in busy streets, to the detriment of public transport operations. *N. N. Forbes*

should continue to control traffic at peak periods; as to the signals, the cycle of lights should be speeded up to reduce traffic delay and they should be switched off altogether after the evening rush. Other measures to alleviate the situation, apart from limitations on parking, included a system of one-way streets, and the segregation of traffic in order to leave certain streets free for the exclusive use of public passenger vehicles.

Marks never tired of urging the need for priority to be given to public transport in the city. He pointed to the peak period tramcar passing through the city centre carrying an average of some 50 passengers, while at the same time private motor cars on the same streets were each carrying an average of about $1\frac{1}{2}$ persons. 'Can anybody justify the cry', he asked, 'that the public passenger transport vehicles should be moved into back streets or should be kept away from the centre of the city in order to accommodate that very small minority?'

It had been suggested that trams should be withdrawn from the centre of the city within a radius of about $1\frac{1}{2}$ miles of Pier Head; termini would be outside this area, and passengers would change to buses to complete their journeys into the central district. This idea Marks condemned as 'absurd, wrong and unjust'. If passengers had to change vehicles, this would add to their journey time, cause considerable annoyance to them, and involve substantial expense in the provision of the necessary shelters and sidings at the interchange points, where space was just not available anyway.

Two basic conclusions emerged from Marks' report. First, 'in view of the vast majority of the street users being passengers in public service vehicles, they should be given every possible facility for free and easy passage along the streets, especially at peak periods'. The second conclusion was both farsighted and realistic: 'Ultimately costly schemes will have to be considered, such as the construction of new thoroughfares and the widening of present main streets. Such schemes, besides being costly, take much time to develop, and should only be considered after close examination of any improvement which can be made to the usage of present street accommodation'.

Staggering of working hours as a means of easing the rush-hour problem was being advocated during the 1930s, as it has been proposed before and since, at all times with generally little success. Referring specifically to industrial development at Speke where some 5,000 workers would be employed, Marks in 1938 described the problems of transporting large numbers of people to and from the same place at the same time; they had to be carried to the factories from all parts of the city, and of course none of them wanted to arrive at work any earlier than they had to. Bus services needed to be duplicated in order that everyone could arrive about two minutes before the eight o'clock starting time, while the earlier services were simply not used. Some form of staggering would save both trouble and expense to the Transport Department, but Marks had found that both employers and employees were reluctant to consider the idea. As he saw it, only two remedies existed: staggered hours or higher fares. 'Will it be better', he asked, 'for the workpeople to face an increase of fares in order to make the provision of transport an economic proposition, or to arrive at their work a quarter of an hour or half an hour earlier than at present and finish earlier?' Similar conditions prevailed in what amounted to another distinctive local 'industry'; two flourishing football pool firms between them employed about 7,000 girls, most of whom required to travel to and from their work by public transport, including special Corporation buses.

# 5 Over the Water

## Crossing the Mersey

*This narrow strip of land, rich, fertile and full of inhabitants, is called Wirall, or by some Wirehall. Here is a ferry over the Mersey, which at full sea is more than two miles over.*
Daniel Defoe, A Tour Through England and Wales, 1724

The Wirral Peninsula is 'an ideal place for residence by business people', the Edwardian guide book tells us. It is 'easily reached from busy towns, and provides all the attractions of the sea coast, with beautiful country inland'. Whether you want to indulge in walking, golfing or yachting, you will find all you need, with the advantages of 'bracing sea air, good sands and bathing, efficient sanitation and good water'. For members of 'the commercial world of Liverpool and Birkenhead' there are fast trains morning and evening, and season ticket rates are 'very reasonable'.

Birkenhead, with its docks and shipyards, was the focus of 19th century growth. Poor communications still kept most of the peninsula relatively inaccessible, a region of fishing villages and windswept sand dunes. Ferries had long maintained the links with Liverpool, but widespread expansion awaited the coming of more convenient through travel facilities; the Mersey Railway in its tunnel gave valuable all-weather rapid transit, the Wirral Railway crossed the peninsula, and, more especially, in the 20th century the ubiquitous motor bus opened up fresh territory, while the private car came through the new Mersey Tunnel. In the era of bus and car, the Wirral became the great dormitory of Liverpool.

While suburban houses spread westward, industry crept southward: past the shipyards of Cammell-Laird and the model village of Port Sunlight, the chemical works of Bromborough and along the Manchester Ship Canal, which in its turn had encouraged industrial development along its banks. The Birkenhead-Chester railway came this way, but it was the motor bus that was to capture the bulk of the passenger traffic in this flourishing market, dispersing it to suburban housing as well as funnelling it towards Birkenhead and Liverpool. These were the roads where Crosville pioneered its buses, and where interaction of company and corporation was to highlight the need for regional coordination.

A fixed link between the two sides of the river was forged when service on the Mersey Railway, given a royal send-off by the Prince of Wales, started in 1886 between James Street, Liverpool, and Hamilton Square, Birkenhead. Later extensions took the railway to Birkenhead Park in 1888 and the branch to Rock Ferry in 1891, followed by extension to Liverpool's Central station in 1892. This brought the route mileage to about four, of which the crucial part was the under-river tunnel. The strategy was well planned; on the Liverpool side the railway tapped the main-line terminus at Central, the city centre and the docks, with James Street located in the shipping and office district; in Birkenhead, it served town and docks, made connection with the Wirral Railway for Wallasey and West Kirby, and with the Great Western for Chester and beyond. Apart from the workaday traffic, there was also a lighter side; Pendleton noted how 'the excursionist who has gone down the breezy river in the *Daisy* or other ferry boat to New Brighton, occasionally goes back through the tunnel, so that he may show his mate, wife or child this successful piece of engineering!'

No more need one brave the chilly crossing on the ferry, endure the fog and choppy waters of the estuary, chafe at delays at the landing stage; instead, a through train, certain, dry, and fast. Little wonder that in its first six months the railway carried $2\frac{1}{2}$ million passengers and was soon handling 10 million a year. But all was not rosy; never profitable, within two years the company was in the hands of the receivers.

Operations were spectacular, if not economic. Steam traction was employed, after earlier thoughts had turned to such alternatives as pneumatic tubes. Massive six-coupled tank engines, with great condensing pipes and outside frames and cranks which suggested collusion between Metropolitan and Great Western designers, pounded through the tunnels, roaring up gradients as steep as 1 in 30 and even in 1 in 27 with their trains of four-wheel gas-lit coaches. Although the engines were supposed to consume their own smoke and condense their waste steam, the tunnels and the enclosed stations soon acquired an atmosphere that became increasingly oppressive. More and more passengers discovered that they preferred the fresh Mersey breeze to near-asphyxiation underground.

Marvels of Victorian technology were doing their

Above: Wallasey ferry *John Herron*, a paddle steamer dating from 1896, makes good speed across the river. *H. G. Dibdin*

Centre right: Passengers disembark from paddle ferry *Daisy* at Egremont landing stage in 1898. Damage to the pier when hit by a steamer in fog in 1926 almost led to the discontinuance of the service, but Wallasey Council decided on a £30,000 reconstruction in 1928. *Edward R. Dibdin*

Bottom right: There were times when the Mersey crossing was not so pleasant: the deserted deck of the *Storeton* on the Rock Ferry service on a bleak day in 1939. *W. B. Stocks*

74

best for the railway; giant 40ft fans toiled valiantly but vainly to clear the air, while massive pumps lifted out the water that seeped endlessly into the tunnel. These machines were kept going by steam engines that ate up coal (and the slender profits) at an alarming rate. Originally the railway company had been authorised to levy a special toll equivalent to a distance of five miles for the use of the tunnel, but the Committee on Railway Rates and Charges had rejected this idea and ruled that the tunnel should be regarded as any other ordinary line of the same length, despite the fact that the company had to foot a bill for some £40,000 a year just to keep the water out. Further troubles came with the advent of electric tramways; by 1901 electric cars, which were sparklingly new and clean in contrast to the trains, met the ferries at both banks, to provide fast services to and from all parts of Liverpool and Birkenhead. The number of passengers carried on the railway was falling ominously: to seven million in 1901 and to less than six million in 1902.

Help was at hand; the answer lay in the latest boost to modern traction: electricity. Considered since 1884, powers for electrification were obtained in 1900 and agreement was reached with the British Westinghouse company to carry out the work in exchange for a substantial shareholding in the railway company. So the transformation came about, with the Mersey Railway becoming the first in Britain to be entirely converted from steam to multiple-unit electric operation. Tracks were relaid and electrified on the conductor rail system, and a fleet of new cars came into use to provide a three-minute service. On a memorable night in 1903 the last steam trains puffed their way through the tunnels, to be replaced the following morning by smart dark red electrics. Distinctly American in style, the new cars had end entrances, leading to first class saloons finished in mahogany panelling and third class saloons in oak, though (as a contemporary description delicately put it) 'upholstery is avoided, the seats being either simply of bent wood or of spring rattan'.

A new British record was set for speed on electric lines, with an average of just over 20mph, and in this mood of optimism the tide was turned. In its first year of electric operation the rejuvenated railway carried more than nine million passengers, an increase of some 50% over the last year of steam traction, while by 1907 the rise was around 100%. By 1909 the figure had gone up to more than 11 million passengers, and by the end of the 1920s to some 17 million. Self-congratulation was clearly the order of the day, and at the first meeting after the introduction of electric running, the chairman expressed his 'entire satisfaction' with the conversion; freed from the sulphurous steam engines, the ventilation of the tunnel was now 'perfect', the train service 'could not be better', and with its new signalling the railway had become the

safest mode of transit on Merseyside. Ambitious plans were hinted at; electrification was to be extended over the Wirral lines, while arrangements were to be made for the carriage of goods traffic from the Cheshire Lines. Although goods trains were never to grace the tunnels, electrification of the Wirral Railway was eventually to come, albeit some 30 years in the future.

This hiatus was to prove a long-standing gap in Merseyside's transport network. Crucial as it was in providing the connecting link between east and west, the Mersey Railway suffered from its limited extent; although the two stations on the Liverpool side were adequately placed, they could well have been complemented by further outlets to serve Exchange and Lime Street stations. Travellers from the Birkenhead bank to other parts of Liverpool still had the inconvenience of a change of train or a change of mode. The inconvenience became even more marked on the Birkenhead side; five Mersey Railway stations served the town itself, but beyond these the passenger had to change: at Birkenhead Park for the Wirral Railway, which remained unelectrified, or at Rock Ferry for the GWR/LNWR joint line.

With the development of the Wirral Peninsula as a popular residential area for people who commuted daily to and from Liverpool, the break of journey was a perennial irritant; the commuter from West Kirby, Hoylake or Wallasey took the Wirral Railway steam train but had to change at Birkenhead Park for the Mersey Railway to complete his journey to Liverpool. Although there was cross-platform interchange and the closest possible coordination of services, the average traveller not unnaturally dislikes break of journey, especially when total distance is relatively small. Further, the business of such resorts as New Brighton as retreats for the odd summer afternoon or Sunday outing benefited from rapid and convenient train services, while in the opposite direction, along the Cheshire bank of the Mersey estuary, areas such as Bromborough, Eastham and Hooton were growing in terms of both industry and population.

Under such conditions, both road services and ferries retained an important role. Although change of travel mode was still necessary for journeys involving the ferry crossing, the bus and tram network on either side of the river permitted the greatest possible dispersion of routes to serve a wide catchment area. This was exemplified at Birkenhead's Woodside terminal, where after the arrival of the ferry a whole bevy of buses would depart simultaneously for a multitude of destinations both within the town and beyond, or at Liverpool's Pier Head where an endless stream of Corporation tramcars traversed the loops. At Seacombe, in order to cope with ferry boats each carrying some 2,000 people at 10-minute intervals, a dozen bus routes converged on the terminal. Such was

Above: Steam on the Mersey Railway: the crew stand proudly by their charge, 0-6-4T No 6 *Fox*, built by Beyer Peacock in 1885 and characterised by outside frames and cranks and prominent condensing gear. Behind can be glimpsed its train of four-wheel gas-lit stock, carrying on its end the destination board lettered 'Green Lane'. *Ian Allan Library*

Centre: Mersey Railway 2-6-2T No 12 *Bouverie* dating from 1887 was also a Beyer Peacock product. The small driving wheels were needed for coping with the severe gradients, while the open cab helped to ensure that the crew did not entirely suffocate in the smoky tunnels. After it was displaced by electrification No 12 found a new life as Alexandra Docks No 9 and GWR No 1211, and was not retired until 1929. *Ian Allan Library*

Bottom: Emerging from the gloom of the tunnel, a train of distinctly American-looking cars typified the new electric era on the Mersey Railway.

Top: The approach to Seacombe Ferry in the 1920s;
Wallasey Corporation tramcars gyrate around their loops,
taxis await their fares, and a pall of smoke proclaims the
presence of the steam ferry. Increasing cross-river traffic
led to a substantial reconstruction scheme in this
period. *H. G. Dibdin*

Above: A summer evening in 1937 at Woodside Ferry;
ahead, boldly labelled, is the 'Ferry to Liverpool', while on
the right is the joint LMS/GWR Woodside station. A
solitary Birkenhead Corporation tramcar, soon to make
its final run, stands amid the Corporation's Leyland Titans
while in the centre a Wallasey Corporation Leyland is on
a through service. *H. G. Dibdin*

Two of the Wallasey ferries in mid-stream around the
turn of the century; both paddlers, *Thistle* (above) dated
from 1891 and *Pansy* (below) from 1896. The toll for the
crossing was one penny.   *H. G. Dibdin*

Left: Casting off! 'Wallasey Ferries' proudly emblazoned on his jersey, an employee of the Corporation's maritime division goes about his duties at Liverpool landing stage in this scene from 1936. *W. B. Stocks*

Below: *Leasowe* approaches the New Brighton landing stage. *W. B. Stocks*

Above: Heaviest of the Wirral Railway's locomotives, 0-6-4T No 13 was designed to cope with the increasing weight of goods trains though it served equally on passenger duties. Built by Beyer Peacock in 1900, it had 5ft 3in coupled wheels. In later days it became LMS No 6849.
*Ian Allan Library*

Right: The Wirral Railway advertises its links with the rest of the country in this Edwardian poster. Ferries and the Mersey Railway connect it not only with Liverpool but with practically everywhere named in the two circles on the right, though strangely no connection is shown with the GWR/LNWR joint line from Birkenhead. Golf is obviously one of the attractions of its territory.

the interrelation between road and river service that each bus carried on its platform a clock-face indicator to show the time of the boat with which it connected. For Wallasey especially, the ferries could maintain the edge over a railway which had to pursue a somewhat circuitous course to reach the town.

A fixed landing stage on the Wallasey side was built at Seacombe as early as 1815; this was later improved to incorporate an extension which could be lowered into the river to cope with the different levels of the tide, but the growth of traffic with the rise of Wallasey as a residential area led the local authority to start a major improvement scheme at the substantial cost of nearly £150,000. Finished by 1880, the facilities were then to serve for over 40 years before the continuing expansion in traffic caused the Council to decide in the 1920s on a drastic reconstruction project, completed in 1933 at a total cost of nearly £100,000.

An important feature of the new layout was the arrangement for convenient interchange between the ferry and the Corporation's buses. A covered colonnade gave all-weather protection to passengers, who could pass under shelter to the ferry booking hall which was laid out to cater for a flow of as many as 500 passengers a minute. A sign of the times was the provision of covered parking space for 200 cars, an indication of the increasing numbers of residents who were now daily making use of private transport; ironically, the opening of the Mersey Tunnel was soon to give them the opportunity to complete their journeys into Liverpool by car instead of changing to the ferry.

# Wirral Railways

*The Wirral Railway serves a district comparatively new, but distinctly progressive, portions of the peninsula showing remarkable growth.*
The Railway Magazine, 1902

When a single line of railway was opened in 1866 from Birkenhead to the fishing village of Hoylake, much of the Wirral Peninsula consisted of marshland and dune, where the wind hurled sand across the track as the train made its four trips daily to the little townships of Moreton and Leasowe. This original Hoylake railway had a short life; there was just not enough traffic to keep it going and it closed within three years. Under new auspices it was reopened in 1872 and extended to West Kirby in 1878. Important advances were made in 1888 when the line was again extended, this time to Birkenhead Park where it met the lengthened Mersey Railway to give a direct connection to Liverpool; at the same time a branch to Wallasey was opened, soon pushed forward to reach New Brighton. A new Wirral Railway Company was set up in 1891 and the original single track was doubled in the mid-1890s, while another branch was opened to Seacombe.

The Wirral developed as both a holiday and a residential area. By the start of the 20th century New Brighton was notable for 'the vast multitudes which visit it, especially at holiday times, no less than 120,000 persons conveyed by rail and river being scattered over its extensive beach on a recent occasion', as one contemporary reported. New Brighton was reached by either the ferry from Liverpool's landing stage, or by train over the Mersey and Wirral railways, either way bringing the delights of the seaside within a few minutes' journey from the congested city. From wind-swept dunes, where it cost the Wirral Railway some £2,000 a year to keep its tracks clear of drifting sand, promenades were built at New Brighton as it developed into a lively resort claimed to rival Blackpool for its attractions. Cheap fares and excursions brought the multitudes.

Meanwhile Hoylake and West Kirby were 'fast taking the position of first class residential and seaside resorts'. House building was proceeding apace and, as the Wirral Railway's *Timetable, Holiday and Residential Guide* pointed out, 'there are good hotels and boarding houses, and abundant opporunity may be found for indulging in almost every form of popular recreation'. Through bookings were available from Liverpool over the Wirral Railway, either via the ferries or over the tracks of the Mersey Railway. For the residential traveller, season tickets were offered at reasonable rates; before World War 1 an annual season ticket between New Brighton or Wallasey and Liverpool cost £3 3s (£3.15), the equivalent of about 2d (less than 1p) per day for the return journey of six miles each way. Since many season-ticket holders (and there were about 3,000 of them by 1908) also travelled home during the midday break, each of their four daily trips cost them about $\frac{1}{2}$d (about 0.2p). For a time it seemed that the demand for accommodation in the area exceeded the supply.

The Wirral Railway was an active advocate of its own cause. The management were alive to the potential of the locality their railway served. 'The growth of the West Kirby and Hoylake district continues to be very satisfactory', the chairman was able to report in 1906. 'The demand for building has been very large, and houses are being erected, so we may expect in a short time to see an increased revenue from that part of the district, and the company will see that satisfactory accommodation is provided for new residents'. At the same time, the growth of Wallasey 'owing to the effective train service, has been phenomenal', and a new station at Wallasey Village was added in 1907. As an indication of the growing activity of the railway, its revenue (by far the greatest

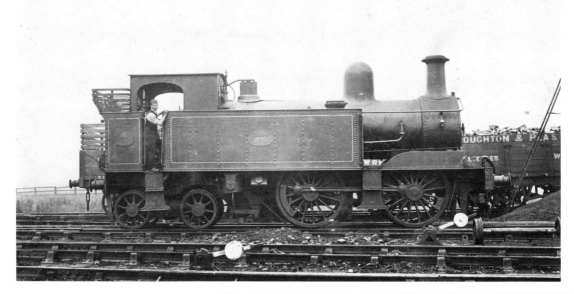

Above: Wirral Railway 0-4-4T No 10 was built by Beyer Peacock in 1894; coal rails have been added to the bunker to enlarge the fuel capacity. Locomotives of this wheel arrangement formed the greater part of the company's motive power, but most Wirral engines were scrapped soon after the Wirral Railway became part of the LMS.
*Ian Allan Library*

Centre right: Perhaps the most elegant of the Wirral Railway's locomotives were three with the unusual 4-4-4T wheel arrangement to ease their way round the line's many sharp curves. No 14 was one of two built by Beyer Peacock in 1903 with 5ft 3in driving wheels.
*Ian Allan Library*

Bottom right: 'On shed' with the Wirral Railway: facing is No 8, one of the Beyer Peacock 0-4-4 tanks of 1887-88. The railway's Birkenhead sheds were functional rather than architecturally pretentious.
*Ian Allan Library*

Above: With steam up, Wirral Railway 4-4-4T No 15 waits to undertake its next turn of duty. *Ian Allan Library*

Below: New motive power for the Wirral: LMS No 15500, the first of a batch of Fowler-designed Derby-built 2-6-2 tanks, was introduced in 1930, when with further members of the class it took up duties on the Wirral section to replace older engines and to form the mainstay of the final years of steam operation. With a weight in working order of nearly 71 tons, it had 5ft 3in driving wheels and carried three tons of coal and 1,500 gallons of water. In 1934 No 15500 was drastically renumbered as No 1. *Ian Allan Library*

part of which came from passenger traffic) had almost doubled in 10 years. 'I hope', said the chairman, 'we are going to be a very big line some of these days'. For a company with only 14 miles of route and 15 locomotives, it obviously nourished lively ambitions.

Effective publicity extolled the salubrious nature of the Wirral Railway's territory. 'Its healthfulness for convalescents, particularly those who are suffering from nerve strain or overwork, cannot be overestimated. In the Wirral Peninsula the golfer finds a paradise, and here likewise is one of the principal convalescent homes for railwaymen'. The emphasis on health can hardly be coincidental in view of the notoriously insalubrious living conditions which still prevailed in the older parts of Liverpool. Family parties not only went to New Brighton, but to the farther shores of the peninsula or the sand hills of Wallasey. Leaving Birkenhead, the railway entered open country, and Moreton station was a popular railhead for many trippers who alighted here to amble along the lanes leading to the seashore to enjoy the invigorating breezes.

Electrification of the Mersey Railway in 1903 suggested similar treatment for the Wirral Railway. Powers were indeed obtained for electrification, but as the Wirral chairman pointed out, his company was 'not in a position to do this yet', in spite of 'a good deal of pressure'. Although traffic was continually increasing and was likely to justify the changeover, the company was still a small concern with limited resources. The problem was a perennial one and was not to be solved for another 30 or so years yet.

Meanwhile the steam trains soldiered on; the Wirral company's black-liveried locomotives were all of the tank type, in half a dozen different varieties, the most numerous being a series of 0-4-4 tanks while the most distinctive were three big engines with the unusual 4-4-4T wheel arrangement. The chocolate-brown coaches were also a mixture, including four- and six-wheelers and bogie vehicles, some of the latter having been created by splicing four-wheelers together in pairs. Many of the coaches had been bought second-hand from the Midland, as well as from the Mersey when that railway had rendered its steam trains redundant by electrification; after suitable renovation they compared favourably with the local trains of even the big railways of the time.

At the grouping in 1923, the Wirral Railway became part of the LMS, again raising hopes that this massive new combine might now have the resources to invest in electrification. Before this happened, though, the new owners made changes in the motive power; the Wirral company's locomotives, as odd-ones-out in the big undertaking, were soon withdrawn, to be replaced by more standardised 2-4-2 tanks from both the former L&YR and the LNWR, as well as by

ex-LNWR 0-6-2T 'coal tanks'. These were followed by products of the LMS locomotive standardisation policy; 0-6-0 tanks came, and then in 1930 the first of the Fowler 2-6-2 tanks which were then to be the mainstay of the line until electrification.

These were not prosperous years for Britain's railways, which were hit by trade depression and by competition from motorised road transport, while the grouping scheme had not resulted in the greatly improved efficiency that had been hoped. Hence major capital schemes required central government aid in financing if the railways were to be modernised to meet the changing future. The Railways (Agreement) Act of 1935 was designed to this end, and in accordance with the provisions of the Act the government approved a £30 million five-year scheme by the 'Big Four' companies; included among the proposals was the electrification of the Wirral lines, for which a strong case could be made on the grounds of improving transport facilities in an area which was not only seriously affected by trade decline, but was also badly in need of a dispersal of some of its overcrowded city population into better surroundings.

Work was already underway in 1936 and orders were placed for 19 three-car trains of saloon stock with air-operated sliding doors. Commuters were soon finding that their local stations were being transformed around them, as new concrete buildings and footbridges appeared and platforms were raised and rebuilt. Since an essential part of the scheme was the integration of Wirral services with those of the Mersey Railway, measures had to be taken to make the two systems compatible; trains had to be able to operate on both the four-rail system of the Mersey Railway and the three-rail system adopted for the Wirral lines, while the new rolling stock had to be built to restricted dimensions in order to fit the tunnels. Some new cars were also added to the Mersey fleet to enable trains to be augmented from five to six cars, and platforms had correspondingly to be lengthened.

In view of the longer journeys it would be undertaking, Mersey stock was prudently fitted with air compressors; hitherto it had been innocent of this equipment, simply taking on a supply of air for its brake reservoirs from a fixed compressor at the terminus. One of the rituals of Birkenhead Park was this imbibing of air; the driver descended to connect up a hose between the train and the air outlet on the platform to enable the car reservoir to be topped up for the round trip. Mersey stock had also been devoid of any means of heating, which had presumably been considered an unnecessary luxury in view of the limited duration of the journey and the fact that most of it took place within the enshrouding shelter of the tunnel. Now that the trains were to venture to the exposed shores of the Wirral, electric heaters were installed.

Electrification and integration come to the Wirral railways: (above) one of the 19 new LMS three-car electric trains introduced in 1938 for through operation with the Mersey Railway into Liverpool. Each set comprised motor coach, trailer and driving trailer, with air-operated sliding doors, and fitted for working on both the new three-rail Wirral system and the four-rail track of the Mersey; (below) the saloon of a driving trailer of the 1938 Wirral electric stock. The patterned upholstery reflected contemporary fashion; note the route diagrams on the ceiling amid the multitude of ventilators and glass lamp shades. *Ian Allan Library*

A 'dress rehearsal' took place on the day before the new services began in order to allow staff and passengers to obtain an inkling of what was in store for them. Then on 14 March 1938 the electric services on the Wirral lines were officially inaugurated, the occasion being marked by an official 'last steam train' conveying railway dignitaries and consisting of modern corridor stock (which had not been standard equipment on the lines) hauled by a cleaned-up 2-6-2T. With due ceremony the 'special' travelled from Birkenhead Park to West Kirby, then back to Birkenhead to traverse the New Brighton line.

The basis of the new pattern of services was effectively a union of the Mersey and Wirral railways to give through running between Liverpool and stations on the peninsula. Electric operation combined with the elimination of the interchange at Birkenhead effected useful reductions in journey time; from Liverpool to West Kirby, for example, the journey was cut from 36 minutes to 29 minutes, and from Liverpool to New Brighton from 27 minutes to 20, representing reductions of 20% and 25% respectively. On both lines the through service was basically at 10-minute intervals in peak hours and 15-20 minutes at other times. The initial arrangements provided that on weekdays the West Kirby line should be served by the new LMS trains while the Mersey Railway trains worked the New Brighton line, but on Sundays both types interworked on both lines. The West Kirby-Seacombe service was withdrawn, to the obvious detriment of ferry traffic.

Thus began an important further stage in the evolution of an integrated transport system on Merseyside. The fast through services of electric trains made the Wirral Peninsula an even more attractive dormitory area, while at the same time dealing a further blow to the ferries; in the first year of electrification the Seacombe ferry alone lost $1\frac{1}{2}$ million passengers.

Southward from the Mersey Railway's terminus at Rock Ferry lay the joint LNWR/GWR line to Chester, with its two branches, one across the Wirral, the other along the Mersey estuary. Rock Ferry was the great interchange, where passengers to or from Liverpool transferred from 'main line' to 'underground', its four platforms and terminal bay presenting animated scenes at busy times. Four tracks continued on through Bebington, Spital and Bromborough to Hooton Junction, past Lever Brothers soap works with its own special station used by the workmen's trains ('The Soap', long formed of antique North London Railway coaches), the workers' dwellings at Port Sunlight, and the growing housing estates which were transforming large tracts of country into flourishing suburbia. The Mersey Railway had its eyes on sending its trains through to Hooton in order to tap this lucrative market, and Merseyside's plans continued to look hopefully at this possibility.

At Hooton, the single-track West Kirby branch diverged, striking out westward towards the Dee estuary, then swinging northward to follow the coast and make a connection with the Wirral Railway at West Kirby. Daily commuters and summer excursionists combined to form the basic traffic over the line as it threaded select residential districts and gave access to sandy shores for picnic parties; some 20 trains a day each way were running even in the late 1920s, though by this time the line's viability was being put in jeopardy by competing bus services. The way was a roundabout one; Birkenhead to West Kirby via Hooton was a distance of 19 miles, compared with the Wirral Railway's direct route of only eight miles. More important, the motor bus came to offer direct services across the peninsula to such places as Caldy, Thurstaston, Heswall and Parkgate, while the opening of the Mersey Tunnel served as further encouragement to the commuter to drive between his Wirral home and his Liverpool business. Integrated development might have suggested projecting the electrified Wirral section services beyond West Kirby along the coastal branch to Hooton and then up the Birkenhead main line to join the Mersey Railway again at Rock Ferry, thus creating a grand Wirral Loop. In the event, the Hooton-West Kirby line was closed to passengers in 1956, by which time the service had dwindled to a dozen trains a day on weekdays only.

Through running from the Wirral Railway had always been limited, but the company did introduce a summer excursion on a Saturday afternoon through from Seacombe, via West Kirby, to Parkgate. Leaving Seacombe at 2.45, you travelled over the Wirral line to West Kirby, reached at 3.08, then over the LNWR/GWR joint line alongside the Dee, 'commanding a splendid view of the uplands of Flint', to Thurstaston, Heswall and Parkgate. Departure from Parkgate was at 8.43pm, bringing you back to Seacombe at 9.38. The return fare for this afternoon out was 1s 1d (about $5\frac{1}{2}$p), but the popularity of such excursions was seriously eroded once the motor bus and the charabanc took to the roads.

Cutting through the middle of the peninsula, the Great Central company's line to Seacombe gave access to North Wales via the Wrexham, Mold & Connah's Quay Railway; opened in 1896, from Seacombe it made its way across the Wirral Railway at Bidston, and then 'the line pursues its course for some dozen miles through the undulating pasture lands on the peninsula'. Early proposals were for trains to connect with Mersey Railway and thus gain entry to Liverpool, and some land was even purchased for a connecting link from a point between Upton and Storeton and into Birkenhead to join the Mersey at Central, but the plans never reached fruition.

Above and right: Integration of
Wirral services: (above) one of the
new LMS electric trains near
Moreton on the West Kirby line,
inward bound for Liverpool Central;
(right) a Mersey Railway train on a
New Brighton working enters
Birkenhead North on three-rail track.
*Ian Allan Library; W. B. Stocks*

Below right: The little station of
Thurstaston on the West Kirby-
Hooton joint line nestles between
rows of beach bungalows and the
gentle Wirral hills.   *W. B. Stocks*

Above: For its part in the working of the joint Birkenhead-Chester line and the associated branches, the LNWR made use of its 2-4-2 tanks; in early LMS days, No 9628 is on the way to Chester with a neat train of ex-LNWR six-wheelers. *Ian Allan Library*

Below: A civic occasion: Wallasey tramcars decorated for a royal visit in 1914 stand at Seacombe Ferry. *H. G. Dibden*

The joint main line to Birkenhead enabled the Great Western to compete for Merseyside traffic. The terminus of its line from Chester, Birkenhead's Woodside station was convenient for the ferries. The Chester & Birkenhead Railway had come on the scene at an early date, opening in 1840, while the extension to Woodside was made in 1878. The Great Western also gained an ally in the Mersey Railway, whose connection at its Rock Ferry station gave close interchange and the alternative of rapid transit under the river; the GWR even sent a few of its own trains through the tunnels for a time, but apparently the operation was not sufficiently successful to justify a sustained through service into Liverpool. Great Western expresses ran from Woodside to Paddington, half a dozen of them making the journey in $4\frac{1}{2}$ to 5hrs. At the same time, the LNWR, while concentrating on its Liverpool services, also offered a few through trains to Euston, the best of them covering the ground in some $4\frac{1}{2}$hrs; facilities included through coaches to and from New Brighton, these being attached to or detached from the main train at Hooton.

Other through services recall the time when the most unlikely workings were initiated, seemingly in an effort to find the most ingenious routes between the most unexpected termini; in the early years of the century such workings were a manifestation of an increasing spirit of cooperation among separate railways, which had apparently suddenly discovered that their lines joined and that outright competition was becoming too unremunerative in an era of shrinking profits. So from Birkenhead you could travel through to the south coast to such places as Dover, Ramsgate, Southampton and Bournemouth. Convenience rather than speed was obviously the principal attraction for the passenger; departing from Woodside at 9.35am, you were due to reach Bournemouth at 5.14pm. Even after the electrification of the Wirral lines, the LMS still ran one steam train a day over the tracks between New Brighton and West Kirby to convey the through coach for Euston. Paradoxically, there was a lack of through services in some cases where they might have seemed an obvious necessity; less than happy in this respect was the line to Helsby, which was worked as a branch from Hooton, where passengers were obliged to change trains. With the development of the district served by the line, especially the rising Ellesmere Port after the opening of the Manchester Ship Canal, the absence of a through service put the railway at a disadvantage and offered an opening to the motor bus.

One sidelight of competition between the railway companies would have given delight to the enthusiast if to no one else. The fare offered by the LNWR between Liverpool and West Kirby was the same as that on the direct Mersey Railway-Wirral Railway route, in spite of the fact that the LNWR's route between the two

points totalled some 40 miles and involved travelling via Widnes and Chester. So for your third class return fare of 1s 3d (just over 6p) you rode on the LNWR at the bargain rate of five miles for one penny.

## Municipal Tram and Bus

*I remember the first tramway service in this country. That was horse traction at Birkenhead, and I remember as a schoolboy in that borough, taking a cheap ride on the tailboard of the old horse car.*
Sir Archibald Salvidge, Leader of Liverpool City Council, 1926

Birkenhead is recorded as having a service of omnibuses as early as 1849, but it was the opening in 1860 of the American George Francis Train's 'street railway' — the first street tramway to be constructed in Britain — that put the town into the transport history books. Although Train's undertaking met with opposition, by the end of the 1870s Birkenhead had four tramway routes worked by three different companies. The Corporation obtained operating powers itself in 1897, and in due course the first electric cars were inaugurated in 1901. Tracks ran along the line of docks, to Rock Ferry, and to inland suburbs such as Claughton and Prenton.

The string of inland docks served to set up a watery boundary between Birkenhead and its northern neighbours of Seacombe and Wallasey. Bridges crossed at intervals, some of them with opening spans which could play havoc with road traffic when ships required to get in or out. No trams crossed the bridges, and it was not until the 1920s that the motor bus provided effective local transport facilities to link north and south.

Situated at the tip of the Wirral Peninsula, separated from Liverpool by the Mersey and from next-door Birkenhead by the line of docks, Wallasey grew up through the merger of formerly separate villages: Liscard, New Brighton, Egremont, Seacombe. The first tramways were installed in 1879 as a result of private enterprise, and although the ferries had been municipally owned since 1863, it was not until the town of Wallasey received its charter of incorporation in 1901 that the tramways were municipalised, with the first electric cars starting operation in 1902.

With the growth of the town as a dormitory suburb and a seaside resort, the first decade of the century saw a rapid increase in population: from 25,000 in 1901 to nearly 80,000 in 1911. The year 1911 also saw the last extension of the tramways, which by then had played their part in unifying the community by providing a series of circular routes connecting almost everywhere to almost everywhere else. Transport

Neighbouring Titans: (above) Birkenhead Corporation No 139 dated from 1930 and had a 51-seat Leyland body; it is seen here at Moreton Shore before its return journey to Woodside; (below) Wallasey Corporation No 28 was of 1929 vintage and had a 53-seat open-staircase body. Both photographs were taken in the early 1930s. *C. Carter*

development after World War 1 was primarily influenced by the motor bus, the first Corporation service being introduced in 1920, significantly the year in which the last new tramcar was put on to the tracks.

Southward isolation ended in 1921 when the bus overcame the barrier of the docks, and a through joint service was introduced between Wallasey and Birkenhead by the two municipalities. Modest in extent at first, the new service between Seacombe Ferry and Birkenhead's Charing Cross required only one bus, which each operator took turns in supplying for a week at a time. More cooperation soon followed, and the effectiveness of the motor bus in the integration of such services helped to put the future of the tramways in doubt. The need to serve new areas where population was growing (the districts of Moreton and Leasowe were incorporated into Wallasey in 1928) strengthened the case for the bus. By now the retention of the tramways would have entailed considerable expenditure on renewals, so the change to buses was decided upon, the conversion starting in 1929 and the last tramcar being withdrawn in 1933.

Meanwhile, private enterprise was challenging municipal aspirations. The Crosville company, founded as early as 1906 in the rapidly growing motor industry, started its first bus service in 1911 between Chester and Ellesmere Port. In 1913 it extended its route through Eastham and Bromborough to New Ferry, where it met Birkenhead Corporation's tramcars. So began years of confrontation between Corporation and company. Naturally enough, the Corporation (which back in 1905 had successfully opposed the Mersey Railway's attempts to run motor buses) did not relish the idea of Crosville buses running into the centre of the town over its tracks, taking passengers (and revenue) away from its tramcars; it therefore refused to licence the running of the company's buses beyond this point. Equally naturally, Crosville felt aggrieved at being obliged to terminate its buses at New Ferry when its passengers wanted to be taken into Birkenhead and to the town's Woodside Ferry.

Moreover, when Birkenhead Corporation itself obtained bus powers, it also appeared to acquire territorial ambitions which did not appeal to Crosville. The Corporation's Act of 1914 gave it powers to run buses, not only on roads within its own boundaries but also on half a dozen routes beyond, while in 1923 it even promoted a Bill aimed at allowing it to run its buses practically anywhere, not only within the municipal boundaries but outside them as well. This was too much for Crosville, which successfully opposed the Bill. The Corporation tried again in 1926 with a Bill to give it powers to operate anywhere within a 5-mile radius, but again Crosville objected and as a result the two rivals reached a compromise under which the powers were limited to certain routes.

Eventually agreement reached in 1930 between the two contenders established the pattern for future development and marked a step towards integration. Crosville was permitted to extend its own services into Birkenhead to Woodside instead of having to terminate at the borough boundary, while in return the Corporation extended its services to outlying destinations such as Bromborough, Eastham and Heswall. At the same time restrictions were placed on the picking up and setting down of passengers by company buses within the Birkenhead boundary in order to protect the Corporation's local services.

The 1930 agreement illustrated something of the problems arising from the overlap of operations within an area which was ill-defined in the light of the changing transport pattern. The Corporation could logically claim that it should be granted the right to operate services in districts which, while not strictly within its own municipal boundaries, nevertheless were dependent on the town of Birkenhead as their natural traffic focus. At the same time Crosville could claim that it should be allowed to reap the profits from routes which its own enterprise had pioneered and which had stimulated the growth of traffic from new residential and industrial districts. The boundaries of local authorities did not always make sense in this age of the motor vehicle. The mobility offered by the motor bus enabled people to escape from overcrowded towns: the new suburbia was on the march. It was inequitable if municipal operators were not to be allowed to extend their services because their limits were laid down at a time when the horse tramway marked the extent of the built-up area.

At the same time, of course, the municipal authority had a vested interest; its electric tramways represented a substantial investment of ratepayers' money, and it felt obliged to protect these assets from the depredations of outsiders. Why should Birkenhead Corporation permit Crosville to run into the town centre, its buses taking valuable business away from the Corporation's tramcars? But a similar problem arose when the Corporation's own buses started running along the same roads in competition with its own trams. 'Protective fares' were no more than a short-term compromise solution, and eventually the services had to be 'integrated'; the tramcars had to go, in the interests of meeting the new situation. So, whereas the Corporation's tramcars had served compact Victorian suburbs — Prenton, Claughton, Oxton — Birkenhead's buses spread far across the peninsula, to Moreton, Thurstaston, Heswall. The scale of operations was changed, and although the appointment of Area Traffic Commissioners under the Road Traffic Act of 1930 provided a new licensing system intended to take account of the requirements of

Above left: Frontier: New Ferry terminus of the Birkenhead tramways. Single-deck car No 13 waits to depart for the town. Crosville buses for long were obliged to terminate here, debarred from penetrating into municipal territory.
*R.Brook*

Bottom left: Expansion of Crosville operations on Merseyside during the 1930s involved the services of the modern double decker, such as this Leyland Gearless Titan of 1935; one of a batch of six, M20 had a Leyland 52-seat lowbridge body.
*Ian Allan Library*

Above: Wallasey Corporation buses at the New Brighton terminus about 1930; No 9, a Leyland PLSC1 of 1926 vintage, prepares to depart for Moreton while a Titan follows.
*C. Carter*

Centre right: Threading its way through the holiday crowds at New Brighton in the Jubilee summer of 1935, Wallasey No 56, a Short-bodied AEC Regent dating from 1929 and one of the earliest of the type, departs from Seacombe.
*Ian Allan Library*

Bottom right: Wallasey Corporation No 28, a 1929 Leyland Titan TD1, unloads summer trippers at Leasowe Castle in the early 1930s.  *C. Carter*

Above: Vehicular traffic for the ferries at Liverpool's landing stage during the 1920s was still largely horse-drawn, to judge from this photograph, but the volume of traffic was to double over 10 years and the alternative of a tunnel was put in hand. Vehicle ferries seen loading here include the *Prenton* and *Leasowe*.   *N. N. Forbes*

Below: Improving the ferry service: Wallasey Corporation vehicle ferry *Liscard* of 1921 takes a good load across the river. The *Liscard* and her sister the *Poulton* featured a flush deck almost free of obstruction from end to end to allow for easy manoeuvring of vehicles; loading was by means of two hinged gangways each side, worked by steam engines.   *N. N. Forbes*

a wider area, there was as yet no overall control of what was becoming increasingly one region rather than a multiplicity of separate communities.

# The Mersey Tunnel

*It was resolved that application should be made to Mr Brunel for an estimate of the expense of constructing a tunnel under the Mersey . . .*
The Liverpool Mercury, 1827

In its time the greatest underwater roadway in the world, the Mersey Tunnel acted as a unifying link in the area's transport network. But while it connected the Lancashire and Cheshire sides of the conurbation to overcome the natural barrier of the river, its conception also revealed the problems of resolving local differences which threatened to jeopardise its full effectiveness in the regional context; perhaps the most significant outcome of the conflicts was the elimination from the scheme of any public passenger transport services which could have proved a crucial element in the future shaping of Merseyside's traffic pattern.

Plans for a permanent crossing of the Mersey by either tunnel or bridge were being advocated from the early years of the 19th century. Perhaps not surprisingly in the great Victorian railway age, it was the railway that first succeeded in attracting the necessary capital and enterprise to bring to fruition the scheme of the Mersey Railway, opened in 1886, though the financial results were hardly calculated to inspire a second venture. Nevertheless, proposals for a bridge to carry road traffic were again in evidence by the last years of the century, though it was not until the motor age was well under way that the needs of this rising mode of transport became sufficiently pressing as to urge serious consideration of a new road crossing.

Figures for cross-river vehicle traffic substantiated the case for the tunnel. In the year 1901 the Birkenhead and Wallasey goods ferries had carried a total of 380,000 vehicles across the Mersey; by the year 1921-22 the figure had almost doubled to 640,000. But then, with the development of motor transport, came a period of much more rapid expansion, with the total more than doubling again in 10 years. By 1932-33 the number had increased to more than 1.5 million; of these, the Birkenhead ferry carried just over a million vehicles and the Wallasey ferry about half a million.

Much had been spent on improvements, and new vehicle ferries had been put into service in the 1920s. Launched in 1921 for Wallasey Corporation, for example, were the *Liscard* and the *Poulton,* each designed to take a load of 170 tons of vehicles; a clear and unobstructed flush deck facilitated easy

manoeuvring on board, while four hinged gangways, two on each side, were steam-powered for adjustment at the landing stages. Each of these vessels cost some £86,000. In the same year, two more slid down the slipways; the *Barnston* and the *Churton* were built for Birkenhead Corporation at a cost of about £100,000 each; the Corporation followed this with two more in 1925, the *Bebington* and the *Oxton,* each capable of accommodating about 45 vehicles. Meanwhile in 1924 Wallasey Corporation started on a scheme costing more than £70,000 for the construction of a 'floating roadway' at Seacombe to obviate the delay caused by the old method of employing hydraulic lifts to hoist vehicles between shore and ferry at low tide when the landing bridge could not be used; this was brought into commission in 1926. Yet despite the introduction of new vessels and improved landing arrangements, much time could be lost by vehicles in waiting for the ferry and in embarking and disembarking, while severe weather conditions such as fog could seriously interfere with the service.

The respective merits of bridge and tunnel had been examined in a perceptive report made in 1913 by the Liverpool Tramways Manager, C. W. Mallins. While suggesting a tramway subway from Old Haymarket to Pier Head to relieve city congestion, Mallins believed there was a case for taking 'even a more comprehensive view of the whole question of the cross-river traffic'. Although the ferries gave good service, the growth of Liverpool and its environs had been so fast that 'it is quite impossible for any ferry-boat system to deal satisfactorily with the enormous volume of cross-river traffic'. The communities on both sides of Mersey suffered inconvenience by the absence of facilities for both passenger and vehicular traffic, and his Tramways Committee 'might seriously consider whether the time has arrived when the whole of the authorities on both sides of the river should be invited to cooperate in the provision of a highway to connect the communities which constitute Mersey City'. This was of course asking a lot; it presupposed a substantial degree of cooperation among the various local authorities concerned, as well as their agreement to spend a large sum of money to achieve the desired aim.

Serious objections, Mallins admitted, could be advanced to the idea of a bridge. It could prove to be an obstruction to shipping using the Mersey, while if it were to be of any real value in relieving congestion in central Liverpool it would need to be carried some distance inland (probably as far as Lime Street), and this would add greatly to the cost of construction as well as necessitating the intrusion of an unsightly structure into the city. Even the most modest bridge connecting the two sides of the river would still be something of a record-breaker; including the necessary approach

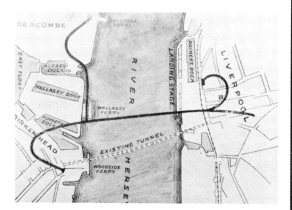

Above: The Mersey Tunnel scheme initially included a branch to Wallasey, but this was later eliminated as a possible obstruction to dock development. The 'Existing Tunnel' shown is that of the Mersey Railway.

Below: Early plans for the Mersey Tunnel provided for a tramway in the lower half beneath the roadway.

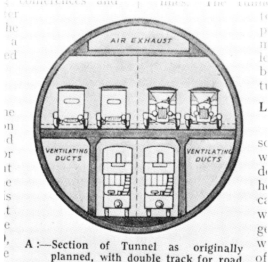

A:—Section of Tunnel as originally planned, with double track for road vehicles above and tramway track below

WILLS'S CIGARETTES

OPENING OF THE MERSEY TUNNEL

Above: Fount of knowledge for many youngsters, cigarette cards sometimes had a direct relevance to local life; this one, in a series on the reign of King George V, depicts the royal opening of the Mersey Tunnel in 1934. On the back we read that on this auspicious occasion 'the green and gold draperies at the entrance parted like a stage curtain, revealing inside the mouth of the Tunnel the glow of an electrically-lit greeting: "Merseyside Welcomes Your Majesties" . . . Thousands of school children took part in the ceremony.'

Below: One of Liverpool's six-wheel Thornycrofts specially decorated to mark the opening of the Mersey Tunnel in 1934. Representing the 'Progress of Road Passenger Transport', the pictures in the windows depict a cart approaching a moated castle, a sedan chair, and a horse-drawn coach, while on the panel below an ocean liner speeds towards a cross-section of the tunnel.
*Ian Allan Library*

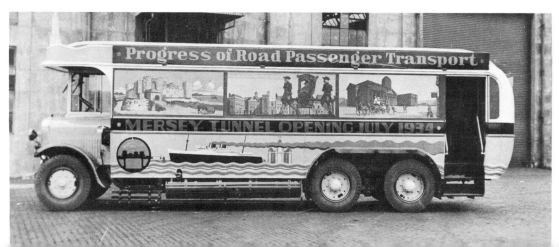

roads, its length would be some 3,500yds, making it about 1,200yd longer than the two famous American giants, New York's Brooklyn and Manhattan bridges. The cost of such a Mersey bridge, Mallins estimated, would be between £5 million and £6 million. To justify expenditure of this magnitude, about 56 million passengers and 900,000 vehicles would have to cross the bridge every year, and these totals seemed unlikely to be attainable within the next few years.

Regardless of whether the crossing was to be made by bridge or by tunnel, Mallins emphasised, there should be 'ample provision for a very frequent tramway or train service, and also for a great volume of ordinary vehicular traffic'. Discussing the alternatives, he concluded that a bridge adequate for the traffic and high enough to minimise obstruction to shipping was likely to be too costly, and he went on to examine the prospects for a tunnel.

Starting point for a tunnel should be the Old Haymarket, from which point it should continue to the landing stage, with intermediate access points. As he had suggested in the case of his tramway proposals, such a subway would also serve to relieve congestion in the city centre. The Old Haymarket was well situated for making connections with Liverpool's tramways, while at the same time it would allow reasonably easy gradients to be incorporated. Going on under the Mersey, the tunnel would come up at a suitable location in Seacombe; if necessary, a branch could also be made to Birkenhead, with an entrance in the vicinity of Hamilton Square.

At some later date the under-river line could be continued across the Wirral to the Dee, with a high-speed electric railway connecting this residential area with the centre of Liverpool, Mallins envisaged. The tunnel should therefore be built with sufficient accommodation for the railway as well as for vehicles and pedestrians, since the trains would have to be segregated in view of their high-speed operation. Mallins thus appeared to put little confidence in the potential of the Mersey Railway, nor in the proposals which had already been examined, and which were at last to reach fruition some 25 years later, for linking the Mersey Railway with an electrified Wirral Railway to provide just such a means of speedy transit.

All-important to any such tunnel scheme was the question of finance. Just how much would the project cost? While careful to stress that his figures were only an approximation, Mallins estimated that total capital expenditure would be more than £3 million. To make it worthwhile, about 45 million passengers each paying a toll of 1d and one million vehicles each paying 6d ($2\frac{1}{2}$p) would be required each year. Although on the basis of the existing ferry traffic he doubted if such a volume would be offering in the first year or two of the tunnel's existence, he was confident that, 'with the

growth of the city and surrounding districts, it would be forthcoming as soon as the great utility of such a highway was discovered by the public'. Indeed, he believed that within a few years it might not be necessary to charge tolls on ordinary vehicles, since the receipts from passenger traffic would probably rise sufficiently to enable the project to show a profit.

No doubt conscious of the problems that would need to be overcome before such a grand scheme could come into being (not least, a reluctance to dig deep into the collective municipal coffers) Mallins concluded with an appeal to local patriotism:
'The construction of such a highway would only be in keeping with the enterprise and progress of the port, and, having regard to the position which Liverpool occupies as second city of the greatest Empire the world has ever known, to which the eyes of the civilised world are always turned, it would be a fitting tribute to her enlightened rulers to accomplish this great enterprise in the second decade of the 20th century.'

As it happened, it was to come, but not until the fourth decade, though in 1914 a committee was set up to examine the problem of cross-river traffic. With the postwar rise in motor transport, the inadequacy of the ferries was becoming more obvious, and in 1922 the Merseyside Municipal Coordination Committee was established, including representatives from Liverpool, Birkenhead and Wallasey, with the object of studying the improvement of transport facilities including a possible tunnel or bridge. In 1923 this committee commissioned an expert report which came down in favour of a tunnel.

The experts considered both tunnel and bridge, and though they had initially favoured a bridge, their views changed in the course of their investigations. Not only would a bridge have cost nearly twice as much as a tunnel (about £10.5 million) but it would not have provided direct access to Wallasey. 'We have unanimously come to the conclusion', they reported, 'that the construction of a tunnel will meet the cross-river traffic requirements, and we have no hesitation whatever in recommending the scheme of a tunnel as the best and most economical solution of the difficulties existing in connection with the traffic across the River Mersey.'

Their report recommended a tunnel 44ft in diameter, starting in Liverpool from a site near the Docks Board office, then going under the river to Birkenhead, where it would come up south of the Seacombe landing stage. There would be two entrances on each side of the river: in Liverpool, one entrance would be for heavy traffic from the docks, with an open approach from New Quay, while the other would be for light traffic and tramways, with an

97

open approach at Whitechapel and along a proposed new street. On the other side, one entrance would be in Birkenhead and the other in Wallasey. The large diameter of the tunnel was chosen in order to allow for the provision of two decks; the upper deck would carry a four-lane roadway, while the lower deck would accommodate a double-track tramway which would permit the operation of through services between Liverpool and Birkenhead and Wallasey. Regarded as an essential feature if efficient passenger transport services were to be provided, the tramway would enter and leave the tunnel by means of steeper gradients than those used by road traffic. The report calculated that the tunnel should be able to carry about eight million vehicles a year, a capacity equivalent to that of Liverpool's Dale Street, while the total costs of the project were put at almost £6.5 million.

After the report, came a lengthy period of uncertainty, during which time the problems of obtaining the necessary finance and of reconciling the conflicting interests seemed to cast doubt on the scheme ever getting under way at all, so that the ceremonial start of work at the end of 1925 represented no mean achievement in itself. Cost was a major problem; while some parties (notably the municipalities concerned) called for a cheaper alternative by the improvement of the municipal Woodside and Seacombe ferries, approaches were made to the Ministry of Transport for government financial backing, supported by arguments depicting the tunnel as a benefit not only to Merseyside but to the whole nation in that it would facilitate the flow of trade, provide work for numbers of unemployed, and bring welcome orders to the steel and engineering industries. Negotiations explored almost every permutation of scheme and finance; the government's first offer to contribute one-third of the cost of the tunnel eventually went up to one-half of the cost, though of a project somewhat modified from the original: both the Wallasey entrance and the tramways would fall by the wayside.

A shadow had been cast over the tramway part of the scheme almost from the start, when the Ministry of Transport's offer of a one-third contribution made it clear that this figure was after the deletion of the estimated cost of the tramways of £1.5 million. Moreover both Birkenhead and Wallasey feared that a public passenger service through the tunnel would lead to losses on their ferries (on which both municipalities had of course been recently investing heavily), and while Birkenhead Corporation eventually supported the tunnel it insisted that the revenue from the ferries should be pooled and that there should be no tramway or railway through the tunnel. Wallasey, on the other hand, came to favour the tramway, though it still wanted to retain its municipal ferry. Opponents of the tramway also claimed that it would

prove impracticable, since not only would it be capable of handling only a small proportion of the number of passengers carried on the ferries (which should have given some relief to Birkenhead and Wallasey) but the fares that would have to be charged to make the under-river route profitable would make travel prohibitively expensive.

If Birkenhead would not have trams coming through the tunnel into its town, then there was no economic justification for only sending the trams up into Wallasey, and hence the Wallasey branch of the tunnel ceased to make sense. Moreover the Mersey Docks and Harbour Board opposed this branch in view of its possible interference with the future development of Birkenhead docks. So Wallasey was out of the scheme, and the tramways were out; as a result the cost was brought down to £5 million, of which the government now promised to pay half. On this basis the Mersey Tunnel Bill received Royal Assent in 1925, and the two partners Liverpool and Birkenhead set up a Mersey Tunnel Joint Committee to bring the project to fruition.

Hopes were high that the tunnel would be opened to traffic by the end of 1928 or the beginning of 1929, but as it turned out this event did not take place until 1934, when on 18 July King George V accompanied by Queen Mary performed the opening ceremony, duly bestowing the name 'Queensway' on the thoroughfare in recognition of the royal occasion. By this time the total cost of the project had risen to almost £8 million. Further controversy had rumbled on about the location of the respective entrances, while an expensive new difficulty had cropped up on the question of ventilation. The original plans, it had been believed, had provided for adequate ventilation, but later experience in America led to a re-examination of the matter, and as a result additional plant costing some £1.5 million was installed; this included the construction of six ventilating stations (three in Liverpool and three in Birkenhead), the bold outlines of which soon made them part of the architectural heritage of Merseyside.

For a few days at Christmas 1933 and again at Easter 1934, the almost completed tunnel was thrown open to pedestrians, and some 30,000 Merseyside people had the opportunity of walking through the first under-water road tunnel to be constructed in Britain since the start of the motor age. Ironically most of these visitors were unlikely to pass through the tunnel again, for it was to be many years before any regular public transport service was to traverse the tunnel. The proposed tramway had been banished, the suggested rail tracks did not materialise, and no bus service was inaugurated. The lower half of the tunnel, which had been specially set aside for public transport, remained disused, hopefully earmarked for the use of motor

Above: So near, yet so far! Liverpool tramcars stand at the Old Haymarket terminus, adjacent to the entrance to the Mersey Tunnel through which they might have travelled to Birkenhead if original plans had reached fruition. Standard No 81 prepares for departure for Litherland in this 1947 view. *R. Brook*

Centre left: A flower of the Mersey: Wallasey ferry *Rose* of 1900 at work on the Seacombe service. *H. G. Dibdin*

Bottom left: The scene at Rock Ferry shortly before the withdrawal of the ferry service in 1939, when both *Upton* and *Storeton* were in operation. *W. B. Stocks*

99

traffic at some future time.

Schemes for bus services through the tunnel did surface from time to time. The municipal operators looked at such ideas cautiously, mindful of the effects they might have on the municipal ferries (in the first year the tunnel was open the Seacombe ferry alone had lost two million passengers) and mindful too of the protection afforded to the Mersey Railway under the terms of the Act. Calculations showed that the tunnel toll of 5s (25p) for a bus, plus 2d (1p) per passenger, would result in an unattractively high fare. At the same time, schemes by Crosville to extend some of its long-distance buses, which then terminated at Birkenhead, through the tunnel into Liverpool were opposed both by the Corporations and by the Mersey Tunnel Joint Committee, on the grounds that such services should be considered as part of a coordinated area scheme, the idea of which was under discussion by the recently-formed Merseyside Coordination Committee. The Traffic Commissioners also inclined towards the idea of coordination, and so deferred the granting of licences. Even a proposed joint service by Ribble and Crosville between Chester and Southport, with protective fares which would have obviated any local traffic through the tunnel, met opposition not only from the municipalities but also from the railway companies, and was accordingly rejected.

In the event, then, not only was there no area board, but there were no tunnel buses. Ironically a short-lived emergency bus service was put on in 1941 when wartime mines in the Mersey brought a shutdown of the ferries, but it was not until 1956 that declining ferry traffic led to the withdrawal of night boats and their replacement by nocturnal buses through the tunnel.

The urgent need for the tunnel and its strategic position in Merseyside's traffic network had been stressed at the time of its construction by the prominent local figure of Sir Archibald Salvidge, leader of Liverpool City Council and one of the scheme's most ardent supporters:

'If you study the geography of this part of the country you will see that Liverpool ends at its river front. If you pay a visit to our Mersey you will see a constant flow of vehicles of all descriptions, down to our landing stage, forming what I call a cul-de-sac, and this traffic, flowing over as it does into our streets, leads to enormous congestion. We are trying to solve this problem. We are constructing under the river the largest tunnel in the world . . . That tunnel will connect the Lancashire side with Cheshire; it will connect with our new Lancashire road which we are constructing right through Lancashire and Yorkshire, and it will thus link up, through the Mersey Tunnel, with Cheshire and the north of England.'

As was intended, the tunnel gave an impetus to road freight transport by facilitating traffic to and from the port. This indeed was its main object; as the official *Story of the Mersey Tunnel* put it: 'the bulk of the business and revenue will derive from the movement of seaborne merchandise and the radiation inland of goods to the south and west from the warehouses and emporiums of Liverpool'. Both steam and motor lorries in growing numbers were hurrying along with their loads on the new highway — and incidentally taking more and more traffic away from the railways.

Private cars in increasing numbers were also flowing through the tunnel. Though car owners were still in the minority, the age of motoring for the masses was beginning, and already Liverpool's Transport Department was expressing concern at the deleterious effects of this rising tide of private cars on the city's public transport. Now the better-off commuter from the Wirral was encouraged to use his car for his daily journey to and from the city, and another attraction was added to the peninsula in its role as a desirable dormitory area.

About three million vehicles a year were expected to use the tunnel during its first years, and to cope with this flow elaborate bylaws were enforced: vehicles were expected to keep in lane through the tunnel, those using the middle lanes were not to travel faster than 35mph or slower than 20mph, while those in the outside lanes were not to travel at less than 6mph. Lights, other than side or rear lights, were to be extinguished in the tunnel, and the use of 'noise-making devices' was banned. On the basis of four lines of vehicles, 100ft apart and travelling at 20mph, the capacity of the tunnel was put at 4,150 vehicles an hour. It is an indication of the continued rise of traffic, as well as the potential of the scheme, that the original figure of three million vehicles a year had risen by the middle of the 1960s to some 18 million.

Success of the Mersey Tunnel encouraged the proposal for a further tunnel in Liverpool, this time to burrow under about two miles of the most congested areas of the city in order to connect the existing tunnel with the new East Lancashire Road. To be known as the Everton Tunnel, the new project was expected to cost about £3 million and was included in a five-year plan submitted by the Corporation for the consideration of the government with a view to obtaining financial support. This project did not materialise, but the flow of traffic through the Mersey Tunnel in the postwar years rapidly increased: from 3.5 million vehicles in the first year of peace to around 10 million in the middle of the 1950s. Eventually another underwater tunnel had to be built, and this finally opened in 1971.

By this time the ferries were feeling the effects of the motor age, though their steep decline did not become to obvious until the end of our period. Indeed, at the time when the tunnel was receiving the limelight, Wallasey was putting into service two new vessels which caused no little stir. Whitsun 1932 saw the initiation of *Royal Iris II*, able to accommodate some 2,000 passengers and setting standards that would hardly have disgraced a cross-Channel steamer; for the first time, cushioned seats were fitted, while the saloons were decorated in 'Old English' style with panels and beams in old oak. One of the painted panels recalled the illustrious exploits of *Royal Iris* which had taken a notable part in the naval raid on Zeebrugge in World War 1 and had been granted the prefix 'Royal' in consequence, an honour now perpetuated on her successor. In addition to the main and shelter decks, *Royal Iris II* had a 'sun deck' which gave passengers more room to enjoy the fresh air and to admire the view in fine weather. A sister ship *Royal Daffodil II* entered service in 1934, making a trail cruise in the Mersey only a few days before the ceremonial opening of the tunnel.

By 1950 ferry services were aided by the installation of radar to help maintain operation in foggy weather, and Wallasey had ordered the first diesel-electric ferry boat. Wallasey too was even looking at plans to extend the services, to link with Bromborough, Eastham and Garston by means of a floating landing stage in mid-stream to allow interchange between the various crossings. Meanwhile the existing ferries were still carrying almost 30 million passengers a year, including 11 million on Woodside and 15 million on Seacombe. By 1970, however, on the eve of the opening of the Wallasey Tunnel, this total had dropped to seven million.

Below: *Royal Iris II* approaches the Egremont landing stage; built in 1932 with accommodation for some 2,000 passengers, she replaced *Royal Iris* and inherited the proud title. *W. B. Stocks*

# 6 New Ways and New Modes

## The East Lancashire Road

*The greater portion of the Liverpool and Manchester road has been surfaced with tar macadam during the past 10 years, but the increase in the numbers of heavy mechanically-propelled commercial vehicles using this road has been so extraordinary during the past three years that the County Surveyor of Lancashire is of the opinion that a still more expensive form of surfacing is required.*
Tramway and Railway World, 1922

In 1898 half a dozen motor vehicles competed in trials in Liverpool to find a practicable mechanically-propelled wagon capable of carrying a load of goods along a public road. The winner of the gold medal offered by Liverpool's Self-Propelled Traffic Association was an oil-fired steam wagon; this formed the prototype for the Corporation's first powered vehicle, which was employed for the carriage of household refuse — not the most dignified of tasks perhaps, but sufficient to signify that the age of commercial motor traffic had dawned.

The big rise in the numbers of motors of course came during the 1920s and 1930s, not only taking business away from the railways, but bringing problems to Liverpool as to other cities. The Corporation maintained a census of the number of vehicles which crossed the city boundary on roads leading to the manufacturing areas of Lancashire; the results showed a startling increase from 1.5 million in 1920 to 8 million a year by the early 1930s.

In 1926 the government approved a proposal for a major new highway between Liverpool and Manchester at a cost of about £3 million, of which the government would provide 75%. Motor traffic between the two cities had so increased that the existing road was estimated to be carrying more than five million tons a year, yet it had to encounter such bottlenecks as a section at Warrington only 15ft wide. The new highway — the East Lancashire Road — would be 100ft wide, and would make possible a considerable reduction in travelling time. Some 20 bridges would have to be built, while other works included the excavation of a cutting through Windle Hill near St Helens.

The origins of the East Lancashire Road were recalled by Liverpool's Engineer John Brodie in an address to the Institution of Municipal Engineers in 1933:
'About 20 years ago when acting as an advisory member of the Committee on Roads to the Road Board, I was invited to consider and report on any improvement schemes in connection with roads between the port of Liverpool and the manufacturing districts of Lancashire, Yorkshire and the Midlands, to which the accumulating funds of the Road Board could be advantageously applied for the benefit of unemployed labour when such a course might become necessary owing to depression and bad trade conditions.'

Consequently Brodie had carried out a study of the public needs, and had submitted a series of proposals including three main trunk roads: a new road connecting Liverpool and Manchester; a new road north from Liverpool, to cross the Ribble and join the main road to Scotland; and the improvement of the road from Birkenhead to Chester. In anticipation of the new Liverpool-Manchester road, which was to materialise as the East Lancashire Road, Brodie undertook the construction of the necessary section within the Liverpool boundary as far into the city as the Old Haymarket, much of the work being integrated with the building of the new suburban housing which was rapidly spreading outward.

The $2\frac{1}{2}$-mile section of the road within Liverpool extended from the junction of Walton Hall Avenue with Stopgate Lane to the city boundary at Croxteth Brook, and consisted of two 30ft wide carriageways separated by a 29ft reservation. Three main routes were available into the city. Two of them followed the imposing Walton Hall Avenue, which was another dual carriageway, this time 150ft wide, and again with a central reservation suitable for a tramway. From here, traffic could travel either via Queens Drive, County Road and Walton Road, or via Walton Lane and Everton Valley, to reach Scotland Road and then the city and (later) the Mersey Tunnel. The third route was through the Norris Green housing estate by way of Townsend Avenue, Queens Drive, Muirhead Avenue, West Derby Road and Islington, much of which was again a dual carriageway.

Above: In deep suburbia: the grass track tramway along Walton Hall Avenue, one of Liverpool's major highways and link with the East Lancashire Road, had acquired a well-established look by the time this photograph was taken during the 1940s with standard car No 137 on service 19A to Lower Lane. Development of the area, including the main road and the tramway, took place during the 1920s and 1930s. *N. N. Forbes*

Centre left: Walton Lane served as one of the main connections between the city and the East Lancashire Road. Its traffic included football crowds, for whom this line of tramcars waits in a special siding, while a bogie streamliner pursues its route to the East Lancashire Road and Kirkby. *N. N. Forbes*

Bottom left: The railways which encircled Liverpool provided obstacles in the shape of restrictive bridges across suburban highways. At Allerton standard car No 314 negotiates the tracks which occupied one half of the roadway under the bridges carrying the main line to Lime Street. *R. Brook*

It was not until the late 1920s that the major project for the East Lancashire Road got under way, with work actually commencing in 1929 on the 25-mile highway from the Liverpool boundary to the Salford boundary at Irlam o' the Heights. Although the distance between the two cities would not in fact be much shortened in mileage, the new road would lead to a substantial saving in time in that it offered a greatly improved thoroughfare compared with the constrictions of the winding way through Prescot and Warrington. The major part of the new road had a 40ft carriageway, a maximum gradient of only 1 in 40, and as straight a course as possible, with a sharpest curve of a gentle $\frac{3}{4}$-mile radius. Although some misgivings were expressed over the fact that a single-carriageway layout was chosen rather than dual-carriageway, sufficient width was available to enable this to be altered at a later stage.

Plans for the East Lancashire Road and the Mersey Tunnel stimulated interest in other projects to improve the road network; indeed at the time it was being forecast that the East Lancashire Road itself would eventually be extended from Manchester into Yorkshire and even to the east coast. One of the most ambitious plans envisaged a 90-mile highway from Birkenhead to Birmingham; the aim was to provide a fast through motor route between the Merseyside docks and the industries of the Potteries and the Midlands, enabling goods to be transported rapidly without transhipment direct from factory to quayside. It was contended that the new road would allow a double journey to be made in the time that a single journey was then taking. The volume of traffic was already held to be sufficient to make the road a viable proposition, based on a toll of $\frac{1}{4}$d per ton-mile.

The proposals included features characteristic of the motorways of 30 years later; the new highway would be 120ft wide, have no severe curves, and be fenced in on both sides. The cost was put at £6 million and it was believed that the road could be brought into use within two years of the adoption of the scheme. Some 10,000 men would be put to work on its construction, thereby making a worthwhile contribution to the reduction of local unemployment; though in the era of mechanised roadbuilding, its contribution to this end may not have been as great as might have been envisaged, if we may judge from Walter Greenwood, whose hero in *Love on the Dole* (1933) watches the building of the East Lancashire Road with mixed feelings: 'A handful of men working, crowds of unemployed watching; "Look at yonder" (indicating the steam navvy), "there use to be a gang o' hundred men every fifty yards. We'll ne'er get work while them things're being used".'

Interest in the Birkenhead-Birmingham scheme came from a wide range of bodies, including the Corporations of Wolverhampton and the Five Towns, the Chambers of Commerce of Birkenhead and Birmingham, the Mersey Docks and Harbour Board, and (perhaps surprisingly) the LMS and LNER railways. However, the motorway age on this scale had not yet dawned, and the government was at this time more likely to give its support to the ailing railways rather than encourage a scheme which would take long-distance freight traffic off the rails.

Meanwhile, to provide a more direct route between the East Lancashire Road and the centre of Liverpool, a tunnel was proposed under Everton Hill, with traffic using a 120ft wide dual carriageway on Utting Avenue. Parliamentary powers for the tunnel were obtained in 1927 and 1930, but because of financial stringency during the years of trade depression, the scheme was still 'in abeyance' when the East Lancashire Road and the Mersey Tunnel were opened in 1934. On the other side of the Mersey, meanwhile, improvements were taking place on the road from Birkenhead to Chester, including a new bridge at Bromborough Port, widening through Bebington, and the construction of the Sutton bypass.

Tramways also came in for consideration of a share of 'undergrounding'. In the middle of the 1920s a tramway tunnel was being contemplated at Everton in connection with a proposed new route from the city to the suburbs. Although the new line through the tunnel would have facilitated communication between the city and new housing estates, its construction would have entailed the demolition of working class housing in its path, and the consequent need to rehouse the families displaced. The cost factor also obviously loomed large in any plans to put tramways underground.

Relief of unemployment was again urged in support of the building of a tramway subway in conjunction with new roads intended to link the two major projects of the East Lancashire Road and the Mersey Tunnel. However, the quashing of earlier proposals to operate trams through the Mersey Tunnel clearly militated against any such project, and tramcars were destined never to go underground.

## Tramcar and bus in Liverpool

*We are still committed to trams, because we find they are the best proposition.*
Councillor A. Morrow, Liverpool Transport Committee, 1937

By the middle of the 1930s Liverpool came fourth in a 'League table' of municipal transport undertakings compiled by *Transport World*. On the basis of the number of passengers carried, Liverpool was topped only by Glasgow, Birmingham and Manchester:

| | Total number of passengers carried in year (million) | Number of Vehicles | |
|---|---|---|---|
| | | Tramcars | Buses |
| Glasgow | 498 | 1,100 | 330 |
| Birmingham | 341 | 830 | 440 |
| Manchester | 334 | 840 | 350 |
| Liverpool | 264 | 750 | 120 |

The comparison brings out clearly Liverpool's comparatively small bus undertaking. (The Birmingham figures included trolleybuses, this city being the only one of the 'Top four' then using this form of vehicle.) Further down in the table, at 21st place, came Liverpool's neighbour Birkenhead, which carried 39 million passengers by means of 45 tramcars and 120 buses, a bus fleet as large as Liverpool's.

On 6 February 1935 Liverpool City Council approved its Transport Committee's proposal 'that the tramways be retained in the Liverpool passenger transport undertaking as the chief method of transport for the present, and that in future any surplus on the transport accounts be not allocated toward the relief of the city rates, but placed in a fund set aside for the purpose of facilitating the possible subsequent alteration of the methods of passenger transport to any other form which may be desirable'. Thus was laid down a policy not only designed to cater for future development, but also breaking with an established tradition as well as going against a growing trend in municipal transport. It was aimed at rectifying the problem of competition between a tramway system in need of rolling stock renewal and a ruinously unprofitable motor bus fleet. At the same time, it had to look to the future when a changing city might need to initiate drastic (and costly) changes in its transport modes.

The proposal was given substance by Council approval of recommendations made in a report by the General Manager, W. G. Marks. A total of 300 new bogie tramcars were to be built at a cost of £660,000 and at a rate of 100 a year for three years, while in addition some 160 older cars were to be modernised. Application was to be made for an Order to authorise the construction and operation of 13 new sections of 'light railways' in extension of the existing tramways. Further, 120 buses were to be obtained at a cost of £219,000 to modernise the bus fleet, and £150,000 was to be spent on new buildings and extensions to depots.

Appointed to the post of Liverpool's General Manager in 1933, Marks had soon set about preparing a report on the future of the city's transport undertaking. He concluded that the retention of the tramways, with extensions and improvements, would be the most economic course to take, at an estimated cost of £1.1

million. The alternative of replacing the tramways by motor buses would involve an expenditure of £1.9 million, while replacement by trolleybuses would cost £1.8 million.

One of the major problems to be resolved was the duplication of tram and bus services. While the city's policy had been to limit its buses to a subsidiary role by confining them as far as possible to roads where the trams did not run, such segregation had become more and more difficult to achieve in practice. Suburban housing developments, for example, required the introduction of new services, and it was inequitable to expect that passengers using these services should be obliged to change vehicles at the point where their bus encountered the nearest tramway. Moreover, there was only a limited number of main roads which could be followed into and out of the city by either tram or bus; elimination of duplication in favour of the tram would again lead to inconvenience for through passengers. From the point of view of the Transport Department's finances, the dilemma was that duplication reduced the revenue on the trams while restricting the buses to a perennial state of unprofitability. The extent of the problem could be judged from the fact that some 50 miles of roads were now served by both buses and trams.

A scheme put forward in 1930 had aimed at overcoming the problem by coupling restrictions on bus services with a system of differential fares. At slack times buses from outlying areas would not enter the city but would terminate at the nearest suburban tram terminus or at a suitable point near a tram route. At peak times buses would operate as usual into the city, but their fares would be revised on the basis of about 1d a mile for the first two miles (trams offered two miles for 1d), then up to $1\frac{1}{2}$ miles for 1d over the rest of the journey. A minimum fare of 2d would be intended to discourage short-distance passengers from using the bus instead of the tram. Transfer fares would also be made available, again designed to encourage the use of tram rather than bus; passengers taking the tram to its suburban terminus and there changing to the bus to complete their journey could have transfer tickets at the same price as the through bus fare. Where both forms of transport were available over the same route, the through tram fare would be cheapest, while a combined tram and bus journey would cost more. Most expensive of all would be a 'luxury' fare for those who insisted on making a through journey by bus in instances where there was also an alternative tram service.

The urgent need for a solution had been underlined in 1930 by Priestly as General Manager. He had pointed out that many of the Corporation's bus services were not in fact providing any additional traffic at all, but were merely competing with the tramways.

Liverpool's tramcar fleet as it was in the early 1930s is exemplified in these two views taken at Pier Head in 1933. (Right) No 234, one of the earliest of the electric fleet, originally had an open top deck but was later fitted with a short top cover; (below) smartly turned-out No 98 was one of the later all-enclosed standard cars. The side destination indicator of No 98, which is working service 43A, is remarkable for the amount of information crammed on to it: 'Carr Lane, Utting Avenue via Robson St, James St, Church St'. During the course of their lives many Liverpool tramcars underwent considerable rebuilding and modification, and it was said that no two cars were exactly alike. *C. Carter*

All but two of these competing services were operating at a loss totalling some £80,000 a year.

Duplication of services was of course by no means a problem unique to Merseyside; it was common to practically every city and town which operated both forms of transport. As buses had to be introduced to cater for growing new areas where it was not practicable to extend the tramways, so the difficulty arose of trying to find them a route which did not parallel the older mode of conveyance. Most operators overcame the problem by getting rid of the trams and running an all-bus undertaking, a process already well under way in Britain by this time. Liverpool, on the other hand, approached the matter from the opposite direction; accepting the principles of the Marks report, it decided to reduce duplication by extending the tramways to cover sections of route from which buses could then be withdrawn. This would effectively 'round out' the tramway system by improving its traffic potential and enabling it to make the optimum use of existing assets.

Implicit in the question of duplication was the assumption that, given the choice, passengers would prefer to travel by bus. The validity of this assumption was sometimes painfully obvious; the bus had emerged as a smart and comfortable vehicle, with the added attraction of newness, while many trams were full of years and were visibly showing their age. Instances were invoked where passengers preferred to wait for the bus, even when the fare was higher. Even in the 1920s, it had been impressed upon Liverpool Corporation that the city needed better tramcars which would offer greater comfort and less noise. Now Marks highlighted the situation by pointing out that of the city's 720 cars, well over 400 (getting on for 60% of the total fleet) were more than 20 years old, while some 150 were more than 30 years old. Little wonder that he urged that the introduction of new cars should be accelerated; hence the order for the 300.

At the same time the Department's bus services were not to be overlooked. As *Transport World* commented, 'it must not be assumed that Mr Marks is monocular in the matter of instruments of transport'. He saw plenty of scope for the bus in the city's transport pattern, including routes where the terrain was unsuitable for tramways, or as a means of relief to hard-pressed tramways in congested central streets. With the recent opening of the Mersey Tunnel, he envisaged a burgeoning of through services between Liverpool and the Wirral Peninsula. Accordingly he recommeneded the purchase of 120 buses over a period of three years. This number of vehicles, it may be noted, represented practically a replacement of the entire fleet, whereas the number of new trams proposed amounted to very much less than half of the car fleet.

The bus fleet indeed seemed to be poised for an expansive future, according to the Council's proposal that tramway profits, instead of going to the relief of rates, should be put into a fund to meet the cost of changing over to a complete bus system. Traditionally some part of tramway profits had been given over to the city for rate relief, a practice in line with the accepted principles of municipal policy. As city councillors argued, the municipal transport undertaking belonged to the citizens of Liverpool, and if any surplus arose from its operations, then they were in the position of stockholders and were entitled to a share in the profits. Over the years substantial sums had been transferred in this way: in 1927 £75,000, for example, in 1928 £115,000, and in 1929 another £75,000.

There was another side to this question of rate relief. Profits were being siphoned off from the tramways rather than being ploughed back into the system to ensure its future. Congratulating Liverpool City Council for 'having definitely forsaken the fetish of rate relief by raiding tramway balances', *Transport World* commented: 'Failure to build up an adequate reserve owing to dissipation of funds in relief of rates has later on entailed calls on the ratepayers for track and equipment renewals, while a conspicuous disadvantage which has been apparent in late years is the inability to change a system of transport owing to the lack of financial balances.'

Now, since the chronically unprofitable buses seemed unlikely to be able to accumulate their own surplus, any profits made by the tramways could be set aside for the purpose of providing for their eventual replacement by buses if this should prove desirable. If this precept appeared to be unfair on the trams, which had already handed over hard-earned profits squeezed out of low fares and were now expected to subsidise their own replacement, at least they gained an extra lease of life while this process was put into effect. They represented an asset which it was currently more economical to retain than to abolish. Nevertheless, the operative words in the Council's motion were 'for the present'; this was obviously a less than total commitment to a mode of transport which might be overtaken by changing conditions, as indeed was to be proved within the next 10 years.

Meanwhile an examination of the relative prosperity of the two forms of transport at this time shows the continued dominance of the tramcars; for 1932-33 they returned a net surplus of £127,000, while the buses turned in a net deficit of £85,000 following losses of £83,000 in 1931-32 and £70,000 in 1930-31. Operating costs per vehicle mile amounted to 13d for the tramcars, but as much as 15d for the buses, while traffic earnings per mile were already 16d for the trams but less than 13d for the buses.

The effectiveness of the plans — which embraced rationalisation of routes, new rolling stock and improved efficiency — would be seen within a few years in a dramatic turnround of the bus situation. For 1938-39 the buses ended up with a net surplus of nearly £38,000; operating cost had been cut to 11d per vehicle mile and traffic revenue had risen to nearly 15d. The trams meanwhile showed comparatively little change; they still returned a healthy net surplus of some £120,000, but while operating cost had risen by 1d per mile to 14d, traffic revenue had increased by little more than ½d, so that the margin of profit was being pared away as the importance of the bus sector grew.

## The Expansion of Liverpool's Tramways

|  | 1911 | 1923 | 1938 |
|---|---|---|---|
| Population served | 817,000 | 917,000 | 983,000 |
| Number of passengers carried (million) | 129 | 208 | 257 |
| Journeys per head of population per year | 157 | 223 | 262 |
| Mileage of track | 116 | 139 | 178 |
| Number of cars | 573 | 630 | 740 |
| Average speed of service (mph) | 7.5 | 8 | 9 |
| Average fare per mile | 0.4d | 0.5d | 0.4d |
| Average distance for 1d fare (miles) | 2.4 | 1.2 | 1.8 |
| Receipts per car mile | 11.9d | 21.0d | 17.0d |
| Operating expenses per car mile | 7.9d | 16.2d | 14.0d |
| Traffic revenue per mile of track | £5,182 | £9,692 | £15,911 |
| Net surplus | £38,244 | £37,234 | £120,568 |

An important role in the operation in Liverpool's municipal transport undertaking was played by the extensive Edge Lane works, opened by the Minister of Transport in 1928. Fully equipped for the production and maintenance of both tramcars and buses, it was claimed that Edge Lane was so complete that 'raw material is brought in from the railway siding at the rear and leaves the front as a finished vehicle'. The old Lambeth Road works, although it had been extended, had proved inadequate to cater for the needs of the growing fleet, so a new works was decided upon, to be built at a cost of about £500,000. The 15-acre site in Edge Lane had formerly accommodated the Tournament Hall, scene of many exhibitions and displays, and the foundation stone for the new works was laid in 1926. To ensure the employment of local labour, much of the construction work was entrusted to the various municipal departments, from the Tramways Department to the Engineering Department, and not forgetting the Parks and Gardens Department which was responsible for the effective landscaping in front of the main buildings. In their turn the buildings were the design of the city surveyor, who adopted the 'late English classical Renaissance' style in brick and Portland stone.

Internally the works was laid out for the 'flow' method of operation, already made familiar by 'mass production' in the motor industry but less common in municipal enterprise. Employment was provided for about 1,000 men, and the scale of the plant was such that the body-building shop could assemble as many as 24 car or bus bodies at a time, the body repair shop could deal with 30, and the paint shop could handle 40 vehicles simultaneously. In aggregate there were nearly four miles of tram tracks on the site. Edge Lane was to play a crucial part not only in maintaining the Corporation's fleet, but in producing large numbers of new vehicles to meet the growing demands of the undertaking. As well as car construction, it was significant of future trends that already by 1931 more than 200 completed buses had emerged from the works.

Liverpool's early electric tramcars had included unorthodox vehicles in the shape of German-pattern single deckers, but later designs settled down into the more conventional British double-deck four-wheeler. Then dramatically at the end of the 1920s another unusual design made its appearance in No 767, a high-speed single-deck bogie car with novel features. Priestly had hinted at the new concept in 1928 when he stated that 'very shortly we hope to have a form of street traction in use which will revolutionise tramway systems, and that is a form of road train, operated noiselessly with a worm drive'.

Car design had been criticised as not keeping pace with the demand for greater comfort and speed. In his 1930 report on the city's traffic, Sir Henry Maybury had urged the need for a car capable of higher speeds, mounted on bogies and offering greater comfort, if the potential of the tramways were to be realised. The four-wheel double-decker was not the ideal vehicle for high-speed operation, especially on the sleeper tracks which now formed a growing part of the Liverpool system.

By contrast, therefore, No 767 materialised as a long single decker on bogies which were mounted as far apart as possible compatible with the curves on the system, in order to offer the smoothest ride. The aim was to produce a car capable of operating at high speeds, with better springing and less noise, as well as lower maintenance costs. The English Electric trucks were of novel design in that each was powered by a single motor mounted longitudinally and driving both axles by means of bevel gears. Side valancing half-covered the wheels to further reduce noise emission. The body, described as the 'super luxury' type, had a 'monitor' or clerestory roof similar in style to that used

Above: Inside Liverpool Corporation's Edge Lane works, where many of the Corporation's tramcars and buses originated. The electric traverser ran the whole length of the main shop and provided access to all the tracks.

Below: In later years Edge Lane works increasingly concentrated on buses; here a Crossley-bodied AEC Regent being cleaned is attracting the attention, while tramcar 246 slips in almost unnoticed. *Ian Allan Library*

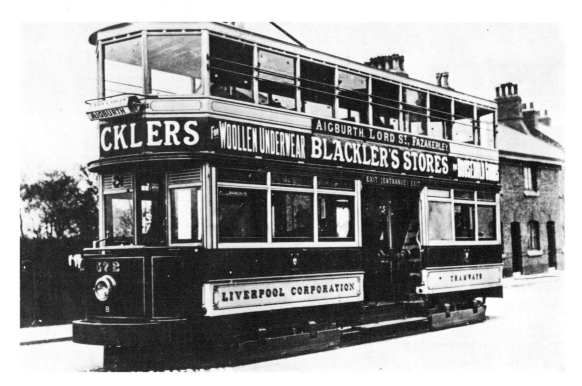

Above: An experimental Liverpool tramcar of 1912 featured a central entrance and exit, with gates and barriers to separate boarding and alighting passengers to and from both decks. Built by the United Electric Car Company at Preston, No 572 had seating accommodation for 84, but the design did not prove sufficiently successful for it to be perpetuated in further cars. *N. N. Forbes*

Below: Liverpool Tramways' unique No 767, precursor of a single-deck coupled-car fleet that never was. The clerestory roof was typical of the Corporation's bus design of the time, while the valancing over the wheels aimed at reducing the perennial problem of noise. Watched here by a youthful 'spotter', No 767 departs with a good load for Aintree; a notice in the saloon window exhorts you to 'Take this Car for the Races'. *N. N. Forbes*

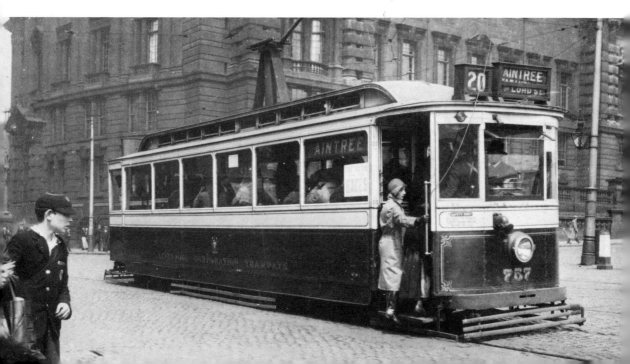

on the Corporation's single-deck buses. Seats were provided for 44 passengers, and a contemporary description of the saloon recalls the opulent finish then still being expended on even the humble tramway car: 'The inside finish is of mahogany, suitably stained and cellulosed in the natural grain... The ceilings are of three-ply bird's-eye maple veneer panelled out with mahogany mouldings and ornamented with gilt lines.'

Seats were of the transverse type, upholstered in blue leather, while the light fittings consisted of 'large base holders with super-lux white glass shades and silvalux opal gas-filled lamps.'

Not the least intriguing feature of No 767 was that its controllers were so arranged that two cars could operate coupled together as a twin unit driven from either end — 'the road train' hinted at by Priestly. The city's reserved-track routes could therefore have been served by high-speed two-car trains, thus exploiting further the potential offered by the segregated light railway layout. As it turned out, this was not to be; while suburban tracks might have favoured the trains, they would not have been so welcome in the city centre, where congestion was a growing problem. Two single-deck cars with a combined capacity of little more than could be attained with one double-decker did not look like proving the answer to restricted street space, while prospects of high-speed working through the Mersey Tunnel to serve the Wirral had already been quashed.

Experience with the new trucks led to the purchase of more of a similar type, but this time they were placed under double-deck bodies built at the Corporation's Edge Lane works, so producing the large-capacity bogie vehicle which the system badly needed. With accommodation for 70 passengers 'on comfortably upholstered seats' the new body, while owing an obvious debt to the Corporation's traditional designs, had fully enclosed ends. Again with the object of reducing noise, the trucks were almost completely covered by removable guard plates, while again to ensure stable running at high speed the trucks were mounted as far apart as possible in order to maximise the wheelbase.

In 1932 a Special Committee appointed to consider transport policy recommended that 'the renewal of old tramcars be discontinued, and that these cars be replaced by new tramcars'. Some refurbishing had been taking place, with embellishments such as vestibuled platforms and cushioned seats being applied to a number of veterans. But such a policy could be little better than a stopgap, and the potential of the tramways could only be realised if improved rolling stock were provided. In fact, a new design of bogie car was already under way, and with its appearance in 1933 came a revised colour scheme: instead of the

traditional red, a livery of 'rich privet green' was set off with a streamline effect on dash and top deck canopy. A dozen of the newcomers were 66 seaters, while a further 18 were slightly longer and seated 70 with the additional feature of a partitioned-off driving compartment. Further variations followed and the re-equipping of the system with the modern high-capacity cars it needed was now well under way.

The apotheosis of car design was reached with the introduction of the 'Streamliners' in 1936. Evolved from their various predecessors, they incorporated what the contemporary press described as "an attractive external appearance, obtained by restrained streamlining of the ends, together with shaped vestibule windows'. Four-motor equipment with electro-pneumatic control, mostly with EMB trucks, inspired lively performance adapted to both the frequent stoppages of in-town street running and the faster suburban sleeper tracks. Leather upholstered seats accommodated 78 passengers, 34 in the lower saloon and 44 in the upper. A total of 163 bogie streamliners of the type were built, while in 1938 a four-wheel version — which came to be known as the 'Baby Grands' — was introduced, and the last of these did not come on to the tracks until 1942. They were to prove to be Liverpool's last new tramcars.

At the same time the Liverpool bus fleet was being revolutionised. Instead of the city's own individualistic designs, turned out by craftsmen at Edge Lane, standard mass-produced models from the AEC works were taking the lead, so that the city's buses began to conform to a general pattern of standardisation during this period. But standardisation had its great economic merits in reducing the costs of maintenance, and cost reduction was also effected by the advent of the diesel engine as motive power. Marks was able to report early in 1936 that experience during the past few months with the department's new diesel-engined buses revealed that their operating costs amounted to less than 10d per vehicle mile, compared with more than 13d for the petrol-engined vehicles. This was a welcome discovery at a juncture when revenue earned by the buses came to less than 13d per vehicle mile. Not surprisingly, Marks recommended a repeat order for another 40 AEC diesels.

And what about the buses of the other Merseyside municipalities? Here as in Liverpool there was a period of rapid development during the 1930s. In the year 1930 Birkenhead Corporation owned 117 buses, Wallasey 62, Southport 22 and St Helens 21. All these towns still had their tramcars: 65 in Birkenhead, 69 in Wallasey, 43 in Southport, and 32 in St Helens, which also possessed 10 trolleybuses. By the end of the 1930s the trams had gone and the bus fleets had grown to 177 vehicles in Birkenhead, 96 in Wallasey, 49 in Southport and 38 in St Helens. The number of trolley-

Above: A forerunner of the new tramcar age, No 775, one of the 1933 bogie cars on EMB trucks, leads a line of cars around the north loop at the Pier Head. *C. Carter*

Below: 'Cabin' car No 788 of 1934 at Pier Head when new in its shining streamlined green livery with 'Liverpool Corporation Tramways' and the city crest emblazoned on its side. Note also the informative side indicator; the dignified painted advertisement also gets it message across. *C. Carter*

Top: Tramway modernisation in action: 'Green Goddess' bogie streamliners of the 1930s dominate the Pier Head loops. *R. Brook*

Above: The ultimate in Liverpool tramcar design; 'Baby Grand' No 252, of the type that survived to the last days of the tramways. *C. Carter*

Above: Municipal bus fleets were expanding during the 1930s. Southport Corporation No 25, a Leyland-bodied Titan TD2 of 1932. *Leyland Motors*

Below: The age of the streamlined bus arrives: new in 1933, Birkenhead Corporation's No 185 was the town's only representative of the side-engined AEC Q type. It had a Metropolitan-Cammell 59-seat front-entrance body. *Ian Allan Library*

buses in St Helens, still the only member of the group to run this mode of transport, had risen to 55.

The figures served to highlight the individuality and separateness of their respective operators; within the area were five different municipal operators, not to mention two major companies, plus of course the various railways. Perhaps not surprisingly, some thoughts turned from time to time towards the prospects of bringing all these interests within the aegis of one overall body.

# An Area Board?

*Negotiations are proceeding to arrange between the Lancashire United Tramways, Liverpool Corporation, Manchester Corporation and the New St Helens Tramways Company for a clearing house system, so that through booking may be offered.*
Tramway and Railway World, 1906

Before World War 1 Liverpool's Tramways Manager Mallins had hinted at the merits of cooperation among the different authorities on Merseyside; he saw that the full effectiveness of the transport network could only be realised on the basis of coordination, and in particular he contended that all the parties concerned on both sides of the river should be 'invited to cooperate' on the provision of a tunnel or bridge which he foresaw as a physical unifying force. Time was to show that events were leading in this direction, albeit that progress was sometimes hesitant; indeed much of the story of the region's transport during our half-century reveals the growing movement toward coordination, although for long it stopped short of accepting the idea of an overall area authority which was under consideration more or less seriously over a lengthy period. The relations between Corporation and company in Birkenhead were an illustration of the process; another example was also to be seen on Liverpool's doorstep, in Bootle.

Next-door neighbour to Liverpool, the County Borough of Bootle did not operate its own transport services, but its territory proved to be a jousting ground for those who did or did not want to provide the necessary facilities. Bootle installed horse tramways in 1882, but it leased them to the Liverpool United Tramways and Omnibus Company, which was operating the Liverpool system and which therefore connected the lines with the city tracks to work through services. With the acquisition of the company by Liverpool Corporation, Bootle obtained powers to electrify the lines as well as to be represented on the Liverpool Tramways Committee, and consequently the first electric tramways in the County Borough were opened in 1900. Routes crossing the borough to

Seaforth and Litherland were worked by Liverpool Corporation as part of its own system. When Liverpool started one of its early motor bus routes in Bootle in 1914, between Seaforth and Walton to connect with the Aintree and Fazakerley tramway, Bootle not only approved but wanted more such routes; Liverpool however had its own ideas about the role of the bus, which it did not intend to employ in competition with its own tramcars.

The situation became acute in 1929 when Bootle granted licences to a new company, 'Merseyside', to operate eight routes within the borough and into Liverpool; however, Liverpool refused to license the company's services within the city, with the result that, while 'Merseyside' buses could still run into Liverpool, only holders of return tickets were permitted to board them in the city. The 'Merseyside' company was acquired in 1930 by Ribble Motor Services, which had been formed in 1919 and in which the LMS Railway had taken a stake in 1929; after negotiations, 'spheres of influence' were agreed in 1931, following which Liverpool Corporation took over the Bootle services and the 'Merseyside' company was wound up.

Nevertheless, all was still not well, for Liverpool Corporation soon found that the Bootle services were not profitable; so, with the blessing of the Area Traffic Commissioners recently appointed under the 1930 Road Traffic Act, it withdrew its buses. Ribble thereupon stepped in and applied for the licences. The Traffic Commissioners proceeded to amaze all parties by handing out the licences to a newcomer, MacShanes Motors; at this, both Liverpool Corporation and Ribble protested vigorously, and went on to take their case to the Ministry of Transport and the House of Lords. As a result, the Ministry ordered that the licences granted to MacShanes should be revoked and granted instead to Ribble, with protection on routes covered by Liverpool's tramcars, and consequently Ribble took over in 1933. In the same year Bootle Corporation promoted a Bill to obtain powers to operate its own bus services; although it obtained these powers, they were never exercised, since the Traffic Commissioners — no doubt chastened by their experience over MacShanes — would have been unlikely to grant licences to another newcomer so long as the established operators were providing adequate services in the area.

Meanwhile the adjacent districts of Waterloo and Crosby had been engaging in their own era of competition. Back in 1900 the Liverpool Overhead Railway had diversified into the road transport business by opening an electric tramway from its railway terminus at Seaforth northwards through the flourishing suburbs of Waterloo and, soon after, Crosby. In 1925 negotiations were under way with Liverpool with the object of connecting this line with the city's system, the

Above: Stanley Road, Bootle, about 1920; the traffic policeman has little to do as the tramcars maintain their stately progress along the middle of the carriageway. The central overhead standards, which also support the street lights, are not yet condemned as a traffic hazard. *H. G. Dibdin*

Centre left: In suburban Waterloo; tramcar No 14 of the Liverpool Overhead Railway pulls into the loop in Crosby Road North. At one time there were proposals to connect with the Corporation system to permit through running from Liverpool, but this never transpired and company buses served these growing suburbs. *R. Brook*

Bottom left: After the replacement of the Liverpool Overhead Railway's tramcars, an NS-type AEC of Waterloo & Crosby Motor Services makes a trip along Crosby Road early in 1926. *H. G. Dibdin*

tracks of which terminated at the other side of the bridge from the LOR's tramway. It was envisaged that through running between Crosby and the centre of Liverpool would then be inaugurated. Things seemed to be going well, but then a last-minute deadlock arose over the question of fares, and the talking stopped. Consequently, on the last day of 1925 the LOR's tramcars made their final journeys, and on New Year's Day Waterloo and Crosby Motor Services put on double-deck buses hurriedly acquired from the London General Omnibus Company.

The road through Waterloo and Crosby was also the road to Southport, and these years saw a multiplicity of bus services introduced to capture their share of the lucrative traffic along this thriving suburban corridor. Nor West Bus Services began running in 1927, followed by a rival under the name 'Ideal', while Ribble itself took a controlling interest in Waterloo and Crosby Motor Services; the resulting lively competition led to fare cutting and a superabundance of facilities. Before the end of the decade the Liverpool road was resounding to 14 Ribble buses every hour, plus another 10 an hour representing the combined forces of the independents, Nor West, Ideal and Imperial. Not unnaturally, such an onslaught affected traffic on the Liverpool-Southport electric railway, which responded by such means as cheap day return tickets and a 'lunch hour express' to enable city workers to get to and from their suburban residences during their midday break. A degree of rationalisation was attained when Ribble bought up both Ideal and Imperial, followed soon after by the purchase of the Merseyside company, which in its turn had taken control of Nor West. In the era of the Road Traffic Act of 1930 conditions were different; licensing was taken out of the hands of the local authorities, anxious to preserve their own territories and their own municipal tramways, and put instead under the control of independent Area Traffic Commissioners.

In 1931 corporation and companies (including the interests of the LMS and the LNER which had obtained bus powers under their Acts of 1928) reached an agreement which delineated their respective spheres of influence. Four 'zones' were marked out. In the first zone, which embraced Liverpool, Bootle and Speke, Liverpool Corporation was to enjoy a monopoly of services running entirely within that zone, although the companies were to be allowed to run in from outside. In the second zone, joint services were to be operated under the management of the company, with receipts and expenses shared between company and corporation. The third zone, which extended farther out, was to be exclusively company territory, except where the corporation was operating tramways, while the fourth zone was to be open to both company and corporaion,

with agreement to be reached between the two parties on operations as considered appropriate.

While it served to stabilise the situation, the arrangement did not prove entirely successful under the changing transport needs of the 1930s, and in 1938 a new agreement was reached between the companies and Liverpool Corporation. This defined three areas: services operating entirely within Area A were to be the responsibility of the corporation; within Area B, services were to be jointly operated, while Area C was to be company territory.

Suggestions that integration and control should be carried even further had also been aired. Government-appointed Passenger Transport Commissioners, together with local Area Passenger Transport Boards were being advocated back in 1926 by the Deputy Chairman of Salford City Tramways Committee, Councillor Major John Fitzgerald Jones. He affirmed that the institution of Area Boards 'would ensure that the wider interests of public policy would be the determining factor, instead of self-satisfied inefficiencies in management, and pettifogging parish-pump rivalries which seek to create and maintain artificial boundaries to public travel'.

Speaking for Liverpool as Vice-Chairman of tne city's Tramways Committee, Alderman Frank Smith rejected the idea of such Area Boards as being too slow-moving in an age when transport conditions were changing so drastically. 'There is not likely to be that smoothness of action that one finds when there is a single control, when decisions are made rapidly and can be acted upon rapidly.' On the other hand, Alderman Waring as Vice-Chairman of St Helens Tramways Committee believed that the government and the municipalities 'should take steps for the proper coordination of the municipal transport services'. He was opposed to the encouragement of private enterprise in this field, since links with road maintenance and rates made it essentially a public concern; moreover 'there are patches of country which private enterprise would never dream of touching and which would have to be dealt with by some council or local authority'.

The vagaries of the existing licensing system, which was particularly affecting the municipal tramway undertakings in relation to competing private bus operators, inspired Lancashire County Council in 1929 to prepare a Parliamentary Bill for the creation of a Lancashire Traffic Board and four Area Traffic Committees for the County in order to take over the licensing of public service vehicles from the many different licensing authorities. The Area Traffic Board would be appointed from the Area Committees 'to deal with matters of general policy, and with the licensing of vehicles which operate on routes extending over the district of more than one Area Committee'.

Above: Co-operation in practice: a Wallasey Corporation bus shows both 'Birkenhead' and 'Wallasey' on its indicator; through running between the two towns dated from as early as 1921. No 102 seen here was one of two AEC Q type double-deckers acquired by Wallasey in 1934; they had central-entrance 56-seat Roe bodies.
*Ian Allan Library*

Left: Co-ordination in action: trolleybus interworking between St Helens Corporation and the South Lancashire company. (Above left) SLT No 3, a Roe-bodied Guy BTX of 1930 vintage, at the St Helens terminus of the company's Atherton service; (below left) at the same point, St Helens Corporation No 138, a 1936 Ransomes with Massey body sporting a restrained splash of streamlining, on the short-working over the same route to Haydock.
*C. Carter*

However, the Bill was not proceeded with, for the government announced its own Bill which in due course became the Road Traffic Act of 1930, establishing Area Traffic Commissioners for the purposes of allocating licences almost on the lines suggested by the Lancashire Bill.

Meanwhile, the LMS and the LNER, now armed with general road transport powers, had been seeking coordination with several municipalities in order that their own buses should not be running in competition with those of the municipalities. As a result four joint committees representing railway companies and municipal operators came into being: at Sheffield, Halifax, Huddersfield and Todmorden. But in other cases no such arrangement was reached, and other means of coordination had to be pursued, the railway companies achieving their aims by the control of bus companies within their respective areas; in 1929, for example, Crosville was taken over by the LMS, though in 1930 it was reformed under Tilling and British Automobile Traction in anticipation of the new conditions.

'It is obvious that the time must come when it will be of vital importance for the welfare of Merseyside as a whole to unify its transport system.' Thus ran the conclusion of a study conducted in 1935 by Liverpool University. In the same year, the Merseyside Coordination Committee, a body which had been set up to consider subjects concerning the several local authorities in the area, passed a motion calling for 'an investigation into the possibility of coordinating all forms of transport on Merseyside'. Discussion of such a possibility continued spasmodically until 1938, when three outside experts were called in; they were asked to prepare a report on what was now being referred to as a 'Board' rather on the lines of the London Passenger Transport Board, which had been set up in 1933 with the object of coordinating transport in the capital and which had inspired in some quarters a belief that a similar type of authority would be a good thing in other areas.

When they reported in 1939 the three experts proposed that coordination should be on a 'voluntary and advisory' basis so that there would be no loss of jurisdiction by the existing local authorities. The experts appear to have come up against a general absence of enthusiasm for any new overall body, but they nevertheless concluded that, even within the limits of voluntary action, there was still plenty of scope for cooperation.

One specific proposal they did make was that the transport departments of Wallasey and Birkenhead should be merged; or, as they more diplomatically put it, that the two municipalities should 'be invited to consider the advantages' of a joint undertaking. Such a merger would have embraced not only the buses but also the municipally-owned ferries; no doubt the experts had in mind the pressing need to improve cross-Mersey traffic conditions, for they also urged the immediate trial operation of a bus service through the Mersey Tunnel. The prolonged absence of such a service symbolised the incomplete coordination of the area's transport facilities.

## St Helens and the Trolleybus

*The Corporation propose to apply to the Ministry of Transport for a Provisional Order authorising them to use trolley omnibuses on the Rainford route.*
Tramway and Railway World, 1923

Situated on the edge of the Lancashire coalfield, the town of St Helens had more affinity with the industrial hinterland than with the port of Liverpool, from which it was long separated by a wasteland of 'moss'. But times change; rail and road developments brought new links, and finally, following the Local Government Act of 1972, the subsequent Passenger Transport Executive was enlarged to embrace the town's transport system and integrate it into that of Merseyside.

The first tramways in St Helens started in 1881, and although the Corporation acquired the system in 1897, in the next year it leased the lines for 21 years to the New St Helens and District Tramways Company which went ahead with electrification. Taking over in 1919, the Corporation then found itself the owner of 36 open-top tramcars. Running on single track in narrow roads through the cluster of villages which formed the borough of St Helens, these vehicles were not the most efficient means of transport once alternatives were available. Consequently the Corporation started its first motor bus service in 1923, and then in 1927 the first stage of the replacement of the tramways by trolleybuses was inaugurated, a process completed in 1936, by which time about 40 trolley vehicles were working 20 miles of routes.

Single deckers supplied by Garratt with Ransomes Sims and Jefferies 35-seat central-entrance bodies were the first in the fleet, taking over a 2½-mile tram route between Rainhill and Prescot; reconstruction of the single track to accommodate the increasing traffic would have proved prohibitively expensive, and the trolley vehicle was chosen as the cheaper alternative, with the advantage of maintaining the load on the Corporation's power station. A contemporary description of the vehicles reminds us that the trolleybus of the period still retained something of the tradition of craftsmanship associated with the earlier tramcar: 'the exterior panels are of Honduras mahogany, the back and front being of silver steel beaten to shape ... The

Above: Scenery on the St Helens tramways: an open-top car negotiates the single track in St Helens Road, Prescot. *R. Brook*

Below: The St Helens trolleybus fleet expanded rapidly during the 1930s; here No 143, a Massey-bodied Ransomes of 1936, turns into Baldwin Street on the Ackers Lane service. *C. Carter*

Top: In modernised livery with prominent name and crest, St Helens Massey-bodied Ransomes trolleybus No 150 of 1938 departs for Ackers Lane, past a Bedford lorry typical of early post-1945 road haulage. *C. Carter*

Above: St Helens No 133, a 1935 Leyland, was rebodied after the war by East Lancs. *C. Carter*

Above: Because of its location St Helens became the centre for numerous interurban routes, including operations from nearby Widnes, where the Corporation took over motor bus working in 1909. In early days, the driver poses for this photograph beside his single-deck Commer of Widnes Corporation Motor Bus Service. *C. Carter*

Below: Tram/trolleybus interchange at Prescot; St Helens trolleybus No 153 passes Liverpool tram No 724 in St Helens Road in 1949. A through tram service between Liverpool and St Helens started in 1903 but operated for only a short time. *N. N. Forbes*

interior finish of bird's eye maple contrasted with teak and red upholstery, gives a very charming effect'.

The location of St Helens — roughly midway between Liverpool and Manchester and at the 'cross roads' between them and towns such as Warrington, Wigan and Southport — brought it into contact with neighbouring operators and it is not surprising that through services were in evidence from an early date. In 1903 through tramcars had been inaugurated between St Helens and Liverpool, while in the opposite direction the South Lancashire company connected with Salford and Manchester. These were days when ambitious cooperation was envisaged, and the streets of the town could have echoed to the rumbling of long-distance cars carrying both passengers and freight from Merseyside to Greater Manchester. Although this was not to be, in the motor bus era an extensive pattern of coordination was built up with both municipalities and companies: Salford, Wigan, Warrington, Widnes and Leigh, Lancashire United and Ribble. Schemes included joint working, revenue-sharing, and protective fares on long-distance services traversing the town.

Interworking also applied in the case of the trolleybuses of St Helens Corporation and the South Lancashire company, and the Corporation kept the last of its vehicles running until 1958, the routes to Prescot being the final survivors. West of this point, however, this form of transport did not make many conquests.

In Liverpool the trolleybus received some support from Sir Henry Maybury, one-time Director General of the Roads Department at the Ministry of Transport, who was commissioned by the City Council in 1929 to report on traffic and transport. He believed that Liverpool would be wise not to consider extending its tramways in view of the improvements which had been made in railless vehicles, and he commended the trolleybus for its low operating costs, its high carrying capacity and comfort, its flexibility, and its freedom from noise and fumes. He recognised, however, that with the satisfactory results already being obtained with the tramways, large-scale replacement was unlikely in the near future; for other routes where trams did not run, rather than incur the expense of erecting overhead, the Corporation would do well to concentrate on expanding its motor bus fleet. Nevertheless, in 1930 powers to operate trolleybuses were being sought in a Corporation Bill.

Over the water, Birkenhead's transport manager explained why he did not favour the trolleybus for his town's services. 'My routes are "tail end" routes, practically all of them', he pointed out in 1933. 'They start from the centre of the town, and after 1½ miles of fairly dense traffic the route tails off into very much more scattered areas, and I submit that for conditions such as these the trolleybus is no use at all.' Having reached an understanding with neighbouring operators, Birkenhead was at the time rapidly expanding its motor bus routes across the Wirral Peninsula, while the last of its trams gave way to buses in 1937.

Wallasey had a look at the trolleybus as early as 1923, when an AEC 'railless trolley car' was inspected by members of the Tramways Committee. Contemporary reports tell us that the vehicle 'attracted a large amount of public interest' and a trial trip was made 'without a hitch'. The Council subsequently sought trolleybus powers in a Bill which provided for street improvements and other works, but a poll of ratepayers went against the Bill and it was withdrawn, the prospect of trolleybuses fading with it.

# Airways

*Liverpool is rapidly becoming an important centre of air transport, and already several services to various parts of the country are operating from Speke.*
Meccano Magazine, 1934

During the summer of 1927 a Royal Air Force officer visited Liverpool on a special mission from the Air Ministry. He was to examine a number of possible sites for the construction of an aerodrome, since the Ministry was seriously considering the establishment of a military air base in the area. If this materialised, it was expected that facilities would also be made available for the use of commercial aircraft; it looked as though Merseyside could be on the verge of a new air age. The big air lines gave their blessing; Imperial Airways offered to operate an experimental service between Liverpool and Croydon (London's airport) in order to provide a connection with their cross-Channel routes to the Continent, while the German airline Lufthansa said it was prepared to fly a direct service from Germany to Liverpool to meet the trans-Atlantic liners; by this means, passengers could be rapidly transferred to and from the Continent, thus saving valuable days compared with surface travel.

The choice of the site, which was described at the time as 'practically a wilderness', is attributed to the renowned airman Sir Alan Cobham, and the official opening of Speke airport was made with a flourish; on 1 July 1933 the Secretary of State for Air, Lord Londonderry, arrived in an RAF Hawker Hart bomber escorted by nine Bristol Bulldog fighters. His Lordship first inspected an impressive display of RAF aircraft before proceeding to declare the airport officially open, expressing the hope that before long a fleet of airliners would be added to the fleet of ships operating between Liverpool and Belfast, a sentiment probably not shared by any shipping company notabilities who might have been present. The honour of officially inaugurating services from the new aerodrome fell to a de Havilland Dragon belonging to Blackpool & West Coast Air Services; the twin-engined biplane was brought out from the hangar and was soon taking off for Heston.

A contemporary description of Speke airport, published in the Air Ministry's *Air Pilot*, not only recalls the facilities but gives us an insight into the flying conditions of the time. The pilot coming in to land could be reassured: 'Obstructions are very few indeed; there are some trees about 40ft high on the north-east and north-west sides, and buildings and trees on the southerly side. The roads across the landing ground do not constitute any obstruction to aircraft taxying or landing.'

Safely down, you would find refuelling pumps available, as well as oil and water. If you did happen to have a slight mishap, 'first aid appliances' were on hand and the workshop was equipped to undertake small repairs, while refreshments were available while you waited. The control offices included customs arrangements, but 'prior notification is required for the attendance of a Customs officer'. Flying was normally during the hours of daylight only, but if you had to come in at night, at an hour's notice flares would be put in place, while the line of approach would be shown by red hurricane lamps.

Speke was conveniently situated; an omnibus service into Liverpool started within 150yd of the gates, running every 20min from 9am to 11pm, while Garston railway station was only half a mile away. To provide a suitably up-to-the-minute means of transport between city and airport, Liverpool Corporation put into service in 1935 a distinctive streamlined bus. Based on a Dennis Ace chassis, the 12-seat body was intended to be 'suggestive of aircraft practice', curving down to streamlined ends and embodying tapered wing panels; finished in blue and silver, it carried a winged emblem on each side with the legend 'Liverpool Airport' to designate its special function.

For the remainder of the opening season, operations from Speke included flights to Blackpool, the Isle of Man and Ireland, a pattern reflecting the still youthful days of Britain's internal airways, when services tended to be confined to summer holidays traffic and to cover routes where air travel offered an obvious saving in time compared with surface transport. A glimpse of Speke in the following summer season showed that Liverpool was connected by air with many parts of Britain. Midland & Scottish Air Ferries flew in from Romford (London); passengers continued northward to Glasgow, while interchange was made at Speke with another aircraft for the Isle of Man and Belfast. Blackpool & West Coast Air Services flew to Blackpool, reached in about 20min, then on to the Isle of Man, where arrival was less than 1½hrs after

departure from Liverpool. Railway Air Services, which was to establish itself as the major British internal airline, operated a Liverpool-Plymouth service, a journey which took 3hr 10min by air compared with eight hours by rail; calls were made en route at Birmingham, Cardiff and Teignmouth. The Dutch airline KLM extended its Amsterdam-Hull service across England to Liverpool, so that you could fly out of Speke at noon and arrive in Amsterdam at 3.40.

Soon some of the services continued throughout the winter; Railway Air Services flew in on its London-Glasgow run, as well as operating from Liverpool to the Isle of Man. United Airways worked what was claimed to be the first air passenger service to fly by night within the United Kingdom: from Liverpool to Belfast. As well as the railway companies which had formed Railway Air Services, shipping companies also began to take an interest in the air; the Isle of Man Steam Packet Company formed Isle of Man Air Services in 1937 in conjunction with the LMS and Blackpool & West Coast Air Services, and in its first year the new undertaking carried more than 26,000 passengers, a trickle compared with the numbers carried by sea but a hint of things to come.

Passengers who flew in those days remind us of a long-lost air age. On the Liverpool-Belfast flight, for example, Railway Air Services employed DH86 biplanes powered by four 200hp engines and finished in aluminium embellished with red and green lining; the DH86 carried eight passengers in a 'most comfortable compartment just wide enough to accommodate two passengers abreast in cosy armchair seats', wrote O. S. Nock. Coming in to land you obtained a novel view of Merseyside: 'We came out over the wide inner basin of the Mersey, past Garston docks. Banking moderately we traced out a perfect circle, over the vast railway yard, out over the river again, and so down to make a beautifully smooth landing at Speke airport.'

A note from the timetable of Isle of Man Air Services conjures up an era when air travel was still only for the select few:
'You want to avoid trouble and confusion at the last moment and so do we, and we ask therefore that you arrive at the departure booking office or airport about 10 minutes previous to the advertised time of departure of the service, so that we can deal with the embarkation formalities and give you any other assistance you may require.'

One of the shortest air routes was started in 1937 by a new company, Utility Airways, which provided an aerial link across the river; its 'Cross Mersey Ferry' offered four flights a day in each direction between Speke and Hooton aerodrome, the flight taking five minutes compared with about an hour's travelling on

Above: 'At your service'. The crew of a Railway Air Services' De Havilland Dragon stand by their machine at Speke in 1934. Able to accommodate up to 10 passengers, the Dragon had a cruising speed of 110mph. *British Rail*

Centre left: 'Step this way, madam!' A passenger is given a helping hand to board a Railway Air Services' air liner at Speke in 1934, perhaps bound for the Isle of Man or Glasgow, or even to London to make a connection with the Continental services of Imperial Airways. The big new hangar can be seen in the background. *British Rail*

Bottom left: Filling up: refuelling by electricity at Speke in 1934. The De Havilland Dragon was notable for its low fuel consumption; with six passengers, its fuel cost was only $\frac{1}{3}$d per passenger-mile at a time when the price of motor spirit was 1s $7\frac{1}{2}$d per gallon (about 8p). *British Rail*

the surface. The estuarial location of Speke gave hope that it would develop into an important base for trans-Atlantic flying boats, but as things turned out it was not to play this role. As early as 1928 Imperial Airways had tried a service to Belfast using a Short *Calcutta* flying boat, but the persistent early morning fog of the Mersey too often dislocated operations.

With the continued growth in traffic at Speke (the 90,000 passengers handled in 1935 was more than double the 40,000 of 1934) a major development scheme was soon put in hand. The control tower forming the first section of the main building was officially opened in 1937, replacing what was described as 'an adapted farmhouse', together with a

large hangar, while the rest of the buildings were completed in 1938. Meanwhile, on land adjacent to the airport, a government aircraft factory was being built as the prospects of war intensified; the latest types of military machines constructed at the works would be tested at Speke before being flown off to the RAF stations to which they had been allocated.

Liverpool scored an aviation 'first' in 1950, when British European Airways started the world's first scheduled passenger-carrying helicopter service. Using 4-seater Sikorsky S-51 machines, this operated daily between Liverpool and Cardiff, offering a journey time between the two cities of less than two hours, compared with five or six hours by rail and some nine hours by road.

Below: The age of air freight dawns: packages of sausages by a noted local manufacturer (Richmond Sausage Company, Litherland) are rushed by van to Speke airport and carefully stowed aboard in this nicely posed publicity picture of 1934. Stripped of its passenger seating the Dragon could carry about $\frac{1}{2}$ ton of freight or mails. *British Rail*

# 7 The Age of Replanning

## Roads For All

*The policy of providing adequate street accommodation for public passenger vehicles should have primary consideration, as they provide the travelling facilities for the vast majority of the public.*
W. G. Marks, General Manager, Liverpool Corporation Transport Department, 1936

In 1940 a way was cleared through Liverpool from the docks to Speke airport to allow for the transport of partly-assembled American aircraft; to provide sufficient clearance along the roads, the work involved the removal or resiting of some 70 tram standards and lamp posts, over 100 trees, and 50 traffic signs. Such measures unconsciously presaged the more drastic reconstruction that followed severe war damage, which cut swathes through some of the most congested districts and so opened up opportunties for postwar planning to create a finer city for the future.

The Merseyside Plan of 1944, intended to 'formulate a coordinated policy for the future development of the communities on Merseyside', included proposals for the development of the area's transport facilities, notably the provision of adequate services to and from the port, which was to continue as the focal point of the region's commerce, but also covering both roads and railways throughout the region.

On the road network, the plan remained somewhat cautious; it concluded that the evidence so far available was 'often quite insufficient to justify the expenditure of large sums of money to relieve traffic congestion', and much fuller information was needed. What was clear was that improvements were necessary in order to relieve congestion at certain points, but it gave a significant warning not to expect too much: 'The fashionable habit of suggesting a new ring road or bypass has, between the wars, given us many cases of uneconomic development where, indeed, sections of ring roads or bypasses have proved to be practically useless.'

Turning to railways, the report stressed the necessity for improved facilities for dealing with traffic in the docks area, where plans to this end had already been worked out by the railway companies in conjunction with the Mersey Docks and Harbour Board. Provision also had to be made for catering for traffic arising from the new industrial areas, which had in fact already been located where rail connections were within reach; the prime need was to ensure that sufficient rail capacity was made available.

Development of suburban passenger services, including further electrification, was also recommended. Indeed this was regarded as a basic requirement in view of the proposed dispersion of population out of the old overcrowded districts of Liverpool, Bootle and Birkenhead. Improved living standards, involving a much lower density of population, meant that it would be impossible for the whole of the population to be accommodated within the old urban limits; since many people would have to be relocated outside the boundaries, the provision of improved travelling facilities was essential.

The continued need for cheap public transport, even in the anticipated new postwar era, was envisaged by Councillor G. W. G. Armour, chairman of Liverpool Corporation's Transport Committee, and a member of the city's Postwar Redevelopment Advisory Special Committee. In spite of the expected increase in prosperity after the war, he stated in 1944:
'. . . there will always be, as there has always been, those people who, either through lack of ability or lack of enthusiasm, will live very near the subsistence level. In a big city such as Liverpool we must therefore provide the cheapest possible transport for such people, in addition to providing more convenient and possibly faster services for those who can afford them.'

For this basic purpose, he concluded that 'the modern tramcar running on a light railway in enclosed tracks enables long distance transport to be provided more cheaply than by any other means'. For this reason he believed the city's tramways would be retained and improved; and even if this were not the case, any change from the prewar policy would not be possible for some years to come, in view of the prevailing shortage of buses.

Nevertheless, changes were being proposed for the city centre. Postwar plans included the construction of an inner ring road; this would follow a course from Chapel Street, Tithebarn Street, Hunter Street and Commutation Row to Lime Street and Parker Street, then between Church Street and Lord Street and Hanover Street to the dock road at the Customs House. Public transport would be excluded from the area encircled by this road; the trams would terminate,

Above: The industrial heritage: in Vauxhall Road, Bootle, tramcars share the carriageway with motor lorries serving docks and factories. Postwar development plans envisaged the relocation of industry, with consequent changes in transport demand. *N. N. Forbes*

Below left: Dead end! Liverpool tramcar No 415 with wartime headlamp mask and white-painted bumpers stands at the Litherland terminus of route 28 from Lime Street beside the Seaforth & Litherland station of the Liverpool-Southport line. Postwar plans foresaw drastic road improvements as well as further integration of road and rail services. *N. N. Forbes*

Below right: Tramcar No 846 negotiates the single track to squeeze under the railway bridges in Chadwick Street on the Seaforth route. Postwar plans looked forward to the elimination of such traffic bottlenecks — but such plans were long term. *N. N. Forbes*

while buses would circulate around the road in order to bring passengers within a few minutes' walk of the city centre.

Somewhat more drastic measures were advocated by Councillor Armour, who hoped 'the day will come when the trams can be stopped a considerable distance outside even the proposed inner ring road'. From such terminal points, he believed that small 10-seat battery electric cars on pneumatic tyres could be used to carry passengers into the city — perhaps even into the inner zone within the ring road, since he thought the public would be chary of 'accepting the need for even a few minutes' walk'. On the analogy of the London Underground, however, it seemed 'reasonable to suppose' that passengers would not mind changing vehicles provided the changeover was made under cover and they had only a very short wait for their connection. It may be questioned how far the analogy was really valid, in view of the longer distances and larger central area in the case of London compared with Liverpool; changing vehicles may be more acceptable where many journeys cover 10 or 15 miles rather than four or five miles.

The little battery buses, Councillor Armour went on to suggest, could also have a role in suburban transport. By feeding on to the main tram and bus routes at such points as Norris Green, West Derby or Speke, they could provide 'the luxury of almost a taxi service' along suburban roads for distances of a mile or so at a fare of 3d, passengers being picked up and set down anywhere along the route, a scheme which seems to presage such ideas as the none-too-successful dial-a-ride mini-buses of the 1960s and 1970s.

Banning public transport from the city centre was a proposition that had been condemned years before by Liverpool's Transport Manager. Referring to a proposal made in the 1930s that trams should be kept out of an area within a radius of $1\frac{1}{2}$ miles of Pier Head and that only buses should be allowed within that area, Marks had castigated the idea as 'absurd, wrong and unjust'. However, times were changing. During the black years of 1940-45 the coming postwar world was being envisaged as a prosperous motor-car-owning democracy where everyone would drive their own car ('already chauffeurs are the exception rather than the rule', Councillor Armour had noted). The number of cars was forecast as rising to four times its 1939 level within five years of the end of the war, and obviously serious measures would be needed to cater for this upsurge in material well-being.

Recalling prewar days when tramcars had been blamed for much of Liverpool's traffic congestion, Councillor Armour now exonerated these vehicles, since similar congestion was suffered by all large towns, regardless of whether they operated trams or buses. The real culprit, he claimed — and here he was in agreement with Marks — was the parked car. To meet this problem, therefore, vast new car parks were essential, both in city centres and at large industrial plants. He believed Liverpool 'should seek powers, if necessary, to compel business premises of more than a certain size constructed in the city area in the future to devote one or even two floors to car parks', while the city itself should also provide multi-storey car parks, 'leasing the ground floor to motor traders as filling stations and showrooms'. Motoropolis was obviously well on the way: 'the car-owning public are going to demand door-to-door transport in the future'.

Generous parking facilities such as these would reduce the need for street widening, the Councillor argued, while traffic flow could be facilitated by the introduction of one-way street systems and the greater use of alternative routes to relieve the overcrowded main arteries, all of which measures were to be adopted by the exponents of traffic engineering. Nevertheless, he sounded a note of caution such as did not always accompany dreams of postwar utopia: 'I am far from satisfied that there is not a danger of the planners spending more money than is necessary on roads'. Sentiments of this nature were later to be expressed more vociferously as the true cost of the motor-age city became more apparent.

Postwar euphoria brought with it grandiose plans for the rebuilding of cities to suit the new era; gone would be the old problems of both congestion and overcrowding. On Merseyside, ambitious plans for a new road system were advanced; these included the construction of radial roads and ring roads to banish traffic troubles from the city and its surroundings.

Four radial roads pushing out from Liverpool would speed communication with neighbouring parts of the region: to Preston; to Manchester by two routes, one along the existing East Lancashire Road, the other via Warrington; and to Widnes by way of Speke, including a new bridge over the Mersey between Widnes and Runcorn. These radial routes would be linked by four ring roads. The inner ring road would link the three main railway stations, and public transport services crossing the city would be diverted along it; next would come a middle ring, and then a third ring making use of the existing Queens Drive. The fourth ring would be an outer circle, about six miles from the city centre and already planned before the war. This vast new system would be completed under the Merseyside Regional Plan by further links, including a new dock road, a central area bypass, and connections from the inner ring road to both the East Lancashire Road and the road between Speke and Widnes.

The inner ring road proposed in the new plan was to start at the dock road, take in a widened Chapel Street and Tithebarn Street, pass Exchange station and then make a grand curve to Lime Street, continuing in a further swathe to pass in front of Central station and on to the dock road again. In length it was only just over two miles, and it was therefore 'sufficiently short to defeat any tendency for comparatively fast traffic wishing to avoid passing through the congested central area to ignore the advantages it will offer', the City Engineer explained. As far as practicable, the ring followed existing streets, while its construction would also be facilitated by the severe war damage suffered in this area.

If such bold highways were to banish congestion, no less urgent was the problem of overcrowding, which was the great social evil of prewar Merseyside. It had been tackled during the 1920s and 1930s by the building of suburban housing estates to take the pressure off the crowded central districts. In the postwar world a new word came into vogue: 'overspill'. The County Development Plan prepared under the provision of the Planning Act 1947 envisaged massive migrations of people out of the central part of Liverpool and their resettlement in new homes in other areas; in all, some 100,000 people were expected to move out within the next 20 years. Of this total, most would go to districts on the outskirts of Liverpool; the largest number would move to Kirkby, where nearly 50,000 were expected to settle, creating a new town with its own industrial estate around the former wartime factories. Another 16,000 would go to Maghull, nearly 12,000 to Halewood and 7,500 to Speke. In addition, 10,000 people would go from Bootle and more than 7,000 from Birkenhead. In the event, Liverpool's 1951 population of some 800,000 was already showing a decrease from the 1931 figure of 850,000, but a much more drastic drop was in prospect: to around 500,000 in the 1981 census.

During the interwar years Liverpool Corporation had been pursuing a policy of encouraging the establishment of new industries and the relocation of existing industries in more favourable surroundings. Between 1925 and 1928, for example, some 300 acres of land was acquired at Long Lane, near the East Lancashire Road, and on this was built the Fazakerley Industrial Estate to provide employment for over 17,000 people. Then at Speke in 1929 some 340 acres were devoted to industrial development, to give employment to another 13,000. Such was the success of this policy, that plans were put in hand for developing a further industrial estate adjacent to the East Lancashire Road at Kirkby; this was under way when war started in 1939, when the site was transformed into an Ordnance factory. After the war the Corporation acquired further land to establish an extensive estate for both industry and residential housing.

Such developments inevitably affected the pattern of transport services. Both industry and population were tending to move outward; the new industrial estates were being built adjacent to residential estates. Instead, therefore, of a simple pattern of traffic flows into and out of the city centre, new streams were being established between the factories and their surrounding suburbs, with the consequence that new cross-suburban services were needed to connect home and work. 'Although the city is growing outward', the City Engineer noted, 'the distance between home and place of work is not necessarily increasing; in fact, it is tending to decrease in some cases.' Nor were the workers at the industrial estates necessarily coming from Liverpool itself. The City Engineer reckoned in 1945 that already half the people employed in Liverpool lived outside the city boundaries; during the war in fact some 60% of the workers at the Ordnance factories at Kirkby came from outside Liverpool.

Redistribution of population on such a scale, coupled with the rebuilding of the city, held far-reaching implications for the transport pattern. Back in the 1930s Marks had stressed that, in the face of growing street congestion and its effects on public transport operations, 'eventually it will be necessary to consider the question of wider and more numerous thoroughfares'. Such thoroughfares were now planned; but did they give the same priority to public transport? Marks had urged precedence for his tramcars in the central streets, but now not only were the trams to be banished, but buses were to be diverted around a ring road instead of crossing the city.

And while the proposed roads were to give greater mobility to the city, they were also cutting a way through the old congested districts from which population was moving out; this movement had of course been well under way during the interwar years, but now it was to be intensified, with even lengthier migrations, not only to the utmost boundaries of the city, but far beyond into the neighbouring countryside where residential housing was going up to receive 'overspill'. The redistribution of industry, too, with new factories at locations such as Speke and Halewood, changed the focus of services away from the old narrow limits to intensify problems such as the provision of uneconomic long-distance workmen's services. No longer was the city's transport network the basic penny tram ride within its two-mile radius; transport was increasingly a regional, rather than a local, matter. The wider scale of operations demanded a wider-ranging organisation if public transport facilities were to be properly integrated.

## The Vanishing Tramcar

*Eventually the only relics of Liverpool's once universal tramways will be their grass tracks, enhanced by trees*

Above: During World War 2 public transport had to carry exceptional loads as well as withstand air raid damage and reduced maintenance. At Pier Head in 1942, tram No 771 appears in its wartime guise with headlamp mask, white bumpers, and anti-blast netting covering the windows. *N. N. Forbes*

Below: Continued heavy loads after the war strained resources to the utmost and demanded new vehicles to provide additional capacity. In this 1947 scene a lone tram, already well loaded, prepares to depart from the north loop at Pier Head, while beyond crowds are gathering awaiting other services. *N. N. Forbes*

*into boulevards, running like pleasant green ribbons down the centres of the city's fine suburban radial roads.*
Meccano Magazine, 1954

One of the casualties of the postwar years was the city's tramway system. Granted a reprieve in the middle of the 1930s, the trams were condemned 10 years later when the conditions which had ensured their retention 'for the present' seemed no longer to apply. During the war years, costs had risen while shortages of materials and staff had led to the accumulation of devastating arrears of maintenance. Cars which had already been middle-aged in 1935, by 1945 were superannuated and bowed down by further years of valiant service. The cheapest option, which had favoured the tramcar in 1935, now favoured the motor bus. A report by Marks in 1945 estimated that replacement of the tramways by buses would cost about £3.8 million, whereas their retention and development would involve an expenditure of anything from £6.8 million to £7.4 million. A third alternative, the adoption of the trolleybus, offered a compromise at around £4.4 million.

Although far and away the most expensive, the tramway option nevertheless offered the most comprehensive package, since it provided for the creation of a light rapid transit system based on the reserved-track routes along the wide suburban roads with which the far-sighted planners of the past had endowed the city. In conjunction with road-widening schemes (especially in inner areas) further lines would have been reconstructed on similar principles, while a new fleet of single deckers was envisaged as rolling stock replacement. For years, Marks had spoken out against the cost of congestion, and had argued that priority should be given to public transport in city streets; now that the postwar era threatened even greater congestion, with the anticipated increase in motor traffic, he accepted that the conventional street tramway would have to yield to some other mode of transport, while at the same time he recognised the potential of the light rail system which already existed. However, the private tracks still represented only about one-quarter of the system's total route mileage, and any additional 'upgrading' would have been a costly process.

In the event, as had been the case in 1935, the cheapest option was the one chosen in 1945 when the City Council decided on the replacement of the tramways by motor buses. The cost factors were obviously decisive. But in the background were the plans for the city's new motor-age road network and the schemes for population 'overspill', elements which would lead to changes in the pattern of traffic flows and population distribution, which would in their turn affect the role of a fixed-track transport system

developed on the basis of the prewar route layout. And so the conversion programme got under way in 1948 with everything seeming to go against the trams; even fate took a hand with a disastrous fire at Edge Lane depot. Nor were the financial results at all favourable to the trams: in 1950, for example, they recorded a deficit of £500,000, while by contrast the buses turned in a profit of £100,000.

Performance figures also served to strengthen the case. In spite of the private tracks on which the tramcars had the potential to run at high speed, the replacing buses were able to reduce overall journey times, largely because of their higher speed in the more congested inner areas of the city; on the Prescot route, for example, the changeover brought a reduction in journey time from 50 minutes to 40 minutes, while on the Kirkby route the time was cut from 55 minutes to 45 minutes.

Fast limited-stop services could also be introduced with the buses, a facility impracticable with trams where all vehicles on the same tracks had to travel at the same speed. In 1954 a limited-stop service was inaugurated between Lime Street and Speke, and this was later extended to provide a cross-city link to Kirkby, the through journey of 67 minutes being more than 20 minutes less than by normal service. Other limited-stop buses were put on from the city to Prescot, offering a further saving of 10 minutes, and to the Brookhouse Estate at Huyton. Such operations were of especial significance in improving journeys for passengers travelling the longer distances made necessary by the extension of the built-up area. Moreover an all-bus system made it easier to integrate services, especially when it came to cross-suburban workings or the extension of routes into developing areas such as Speke, Orrell, Croxteth or Kirkby.

In the first two postwar years, a hundred more AEC double-deckers were bought, after which the large demands for the tram-replacement programme initiated a big rise in bus numbers and the fleet diversified with vehicles from Leyland, Daimler and Crossley. The changeover, in the words of the Transport Department, was 'a task of no mean magnitude'; it involved not only the vehicles themselves, but the conversion of seven erstwhile tram depots and the retraining of former tram drivers to take command of their new charges.

| Liverpool's vanishing tramcars | | |
| --- | --- | --- |
| | *Trams* | *Buses* |
| 1943 | 744 | 297 |
| 1948 | 636 | 388 |
| 1953 | 220 | 884 |
| 1957 | — | 1,265 |

Above: Still in grey wartime livery, standard car No 114 traverses Dale Street in 1950. After years of arduous war service, the tramcar fleet emerged in dire need of renewal. *C. Carter*

Below: Conversion gets under way: AEC A35, already replacing a tram on route 4, passes No 765 on service 6 running on the single track in West Derby Street. The street lights suspended from the tram standards recall the traditional link between municipal tramways and electricity supply, a link broken with the nationalisation of the electricity industry. *N. N. Forbes*

134

Top left: Postwar augmentation of the Liverpool Corporation bus fleet began with a hundred Weymann-bodied AECs between 1945 and 1947; among the first of the batch, this one took the number A229. *Ian Allan Library*

Bottom left: Delivered to Liverpool Corporation in 1951 as No A779, this AEC Regent III had 56-seat Crossley bodywork in the revised livery, with the extensive three-blind front destination display necessitated by the rapid expansion of the bus network. *Ian Allan Library*

Above: The St Helens motor bus fleet was strengthened by 40 London RT-type Park Royal bodied AEC Regent IIIs between 1950 and 1952; smartly attired in the town's livery, they featured unusual indicator displays. *Ian Allan Library*

In an article on the transport system of its home city at this time, *Meccano Magazine* neatly summarised the essential facts:
'Every weekday a fleet of 1,100 vehicles runs 107,000 miles, covering 224 miles of routes and serving an area of 77 square miles. It carries daily more than a million passengers. Of these, 350,000 are industrial workers at 2,000 factories and 54 docks; the rest are a medley of schoolchildren, breadwinners, housewives and holidaymakers. The huge wheel of transport rotates to the thrust of 7,000 staff . . .'

A glance at the fare structure clearly shows the tapering scale which was biased in favour of the longer-distance traveller, and if the rate was no longer two miles for a penny this reflected the growing inflation which was to prove such a chronic problem:

| Fare | Distance (miles) |
| --- | --- |
| $1\frac{1}{2}$d | 0.75 |
| $2\frac{1}{2}$d | 1.50 |
| 4d | 4.52 |
| 6d | 6.65 |
| 7d | 8.65 |
| 8d | 10.98 |

# Conclusion

*Transport is one of the dominant vital factors in determining the efficiency of an area for industrial production. The fact that Lancashire's transport facilities have been adequate in the past is no guarantee that they will be adequate in the future.*
Report by Lancashire Chamber of Commerce and Lancashire Industrial Development Council, 1938

One of the historian's favourite pastimes is the game of 'What if . . . ?'; we ask 'what if' something had been different? What if Merseyside's transport had been organised from the start under one coordinated authority? What if the Mersey Tunnel had been built 20 years earlier, complete with public transport linking the two sides of the river? What if the city's tramways had been upgraded to a light rapid transit system? Even if this amounts to no more than an amusing exercise, at least it serves to remind us that transport is the product of circumstances. Granted its influence on such aspects as the growth of towns and the distribution of population, transport is nevertheless circumscribed by factors such as local topography, control and policy, which shape it into its distinctive pattern. In the case of Merseyside we have seen the influence of the river as a dividing line, the effects of competition and cooperation among neighbouring operators, the place of transport in planning and rehousing, the problems of road layout and congestion. Given the circumstances, could the story have been different?

What cannot be overlooked is the ineluctable process of change. However much it might have been ignored or opposed, change proved to be irresistable; the coming of the motor vehicle, the spread of suburbia, the demise of the tramways, the eclipse of the docks and the formation of new traffic patterns all seem inevitable in retrospect, even if they might not have appeared so at the time. And if an apparent reluctance to accept and adapt to change may have delayed what a later age would call 'progress', this may have been due not necessarily to an inability to recognise the extent of the transformation taking place before our eyes, but rather to practical problems involved in discarding valuable existing assets and investing in new projects to take their place.

A particularly crucial aspect of change which made itself increasingly manifest over the years was the broadening of the scale of operations. The wider distribution of population over a much more extensive built-up area was stimulated first by the electric tramways and local railways, and then to a vastly greater degree by the motor bus and the private car. As a result the old boundaries were rendered obsolete; the range of travel ceased to be the two-mile radius of the penny tram ride. Municipal pride had created the municipal tramways within the municipal boundaries, but such boundaries were no longer relevant under the new conditions. Not the least significant factor in the evolution of a regional transport network was the acceptance of the need for a broader outlook capable of envisaging a coordinated system that would transcend the confines of local borders.

If this widening of the transport horizon represented one facet of the transformation which took place between 1900 and 1950, no less striking was the changed environment in which it had to operate. While public transport still remained a dominant element in city life, its pre-eminence was being overshadowed by a new enthusiasm based on postwar rebuilding plans which involved ambitious road programmes and vast population overspill. The electric tramcar, agent of the past urban revolution, was in eclipse, while events were to prove that even its successor the bus had virtually attained its zenith. The future looked bright for a new motor age in which the grandiose highway network of half a county would revolutionise travel habits.

Viewed from the 1980s the transport world of the 1950s looks almost as remote as that of 1900. It is not simply that the vehicles themselves have changed — trams and open-platform half-cab buses are a memory; or that the private car and television have radically altered travel patterns. More fundamental is the enforced realisation that roads are not an end in themselves, and that full 'motorisation' (as Buchanan,

136

Above: Transformation at Pier Head: a solitary tramcar
('Baby Grand' No 289) stands amid the buses which took
over the well-known terminal loops during the
conversion programme of the 1950s.

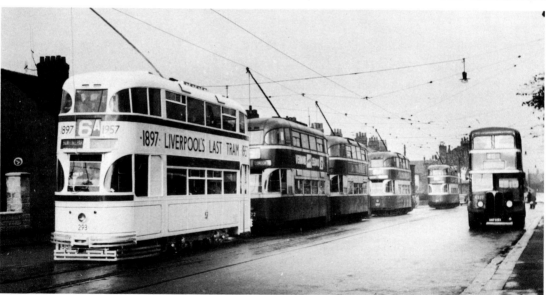

Top: The fate of the 'grass tracks': weed-grown and waterlogged, they are soon to become only ornamental boulevards. Already at Bowring Park, pioneer route of this form of construction, the track has been cut back to the central reservation from its original location within the park in the right background. Here No 264 prepares to return to the city.

Above: Last of the line: white-painted No 293, officially 'Liverpool's Last Tram', brings up the rear of a procession of cars for the closure of the tramways in 1957, while AEC Regent A577 stands ready to take over.

author of the famous report on *Traffic in Towns*, pointed out) is an impracticable and undesirable goal. Liverpool had established a sound tradition of road development which was to stand it in good stead; but, as Brodie (progenitor of the city's modern highways) had shown, the formula was 'roads plus transport': planning had to integrate the needs of transport to serve the great mass of the people. And Marks (rejuvenator of the city's trams and buses in the 1930s) had reiterated the same theme in his constant urging of priority for public transport as the most efficient user of limited street space. Now a later age, concerned with the 'environment' and the call for 'urban renewal' to bring fresh life into declining city centres, has had to concede that the achievement of this aim must involve the support of healthy public transport facilites, even if these facilites could not be justified on the strict criterion of financial profitability. An acceptance of the social role of public transport brings us nearer in spirit to the ideals of those local authorities which, in the earlier years of the century, were running their municipal undertakings for the benefit of the townspeople, in the firm belief that cheap, convenient and abundant local services were an essential factor in enhancing the quality of urban life.

**Merseyside's Municipal Transport**

|  | 1923 |  | 1938 |  | 1953 |  |
|---|---|---|---|---|---|---|
|  | Trams | Buses | Trams | Buses | Trams | Buses |
| Liverpool | 630 | 23 | 740 | 162 | 276 | 813 |
| Birkenhead† | 65 | 23 | — | 177 | — | 227 |
| Wallasey† | 78 | 10 | — | 96 | — | 83 |
| Southport | 45 | — | — | 52 | — | 78 |
| St Helens | 40 | 3 | — | 93* | — | 98* |

\* Includes trolleybuses
† Also engaged in ferry operations

Below: Special tickets for the last trams. The named stages recall not only a past transport system but a bygone era in fare collection techniques.

# Chronology

| | | |
|---|---|---|
| 1774 | | Leeds & Liverpool Canal open from Liverpool to Wigan |
| 1816 | 23-27 October | Ceremonial opening throughout of Leeds & Liverpool Canal |
| 1830 | 15 September | Liverpool & Manchester Railway opened |
| 1836 | 15 August | Liverpool Lime Street station opened |
| 1840 | 23 September | Chester & Birkenhead Railway opened |
| 1846 | | Leeds & Liverpool Canal connection with docks and Mersey in Liverpool opened |
| 1848 | 24 July | Southport & Waterloo Railway opened |
| 1850 | 13 May | Liverpool Exchange Station opened |
| 1850 | 1 October | Waterloo railway extended to Exchange station, Liverpool |
| 1852 | 1 July | St Helens Canal & Railway opened Runcorn Gap-Garston |
| 1855 | 27 March | L&YR North Docks branch opened |
| 1859 | March | Curtis' 'Railway Omnibus' on Liverpool docks railway |
| 1860 | 30 August | Opening of first street tramway in Birkenhead |
| 1861 | 2 July | Train's Liverpool tramway opened |
| 1864 | 15 February | LNWR Edge Hill-Speke line opened |
| 1864 | 1 June | MSLR opened to Brunswick Dock |
| 1865 | 5 July | CLC formed |
| 1866 | 2 July | Hoylake Railway opened |
| 1866 | 16 October | LNWR Bootle branch opened |
| 1869 | 1 November | First street tramways in Liverpool of Liverpool Tramways Company opened |
| 1873 | 2 September | CLC starts Liverpool-Manchester direct service |
| 1874 | 1 March | Liverpool Central Station opened |
| 1876 | 1 January | Liverpool United Tramways & Omnibus Company formed |
| 1878 | 31 March | Birkenhead Woodside station opened |
| 1878 | 1 April | Hoylake Railway extended to West Kirby |
| 1879 | 30 June | First tramways in Wallasey opened |
| 1879 | 1 December | CLC Hunts Cross-Aintree line opened |
| 1880 | 1 July | CLC branch to Liverpool Huskisson opened |
| 1881 | 1 September | LNWR starts passenger train service to Alexandra Dock, Bootle |
| 1881 | 5 November | First tramways in St Helens opened |
| 1882 | 11 July | First tramways in Bootle opened |
| 1884 | 1 September | Aintree-Southport railway opened |
| 1886 | 20 January | Official opening of Mersey Railway |
| 1886 | 1 February | Public service started on Mersey Railway |
| 1888 | 2 January | Wallasey railway opened; Mersey Railway extended to Birkenhead Park |
| 1888 | 30 March | Railway to New Brighton opened |
| 1891 | 15 June | Mersey Railway extension to Rock Ferry opened |
| 1892 | 11 January | Mersey Railway extended from James Street to Liverpool Central |
| 1893 | 4 February | Formal opening of Liverpool Overhead Railway |

| | | |
|---|---|---|
| 1893 | 6 March | First section of Liverpool Overhead Railway opened to traffic |
| 1894 | 30 April | Liverpool Overhead Railway extended to Seaforth Sands |
| 1894 | 1 September | CLC extended to Southport |
| 1895 | 1 June | Seacombe branch railway opened |
| 1895 | 12 June | Liverpool Riverside station opened |
| 1896 | 21 December | Liverpool Overhead Railway extended to Dingle |
| 1897 | 1 September | Liverpool Corporation acquires Liverpool United Tramways & Omnibus Company |
| 1898 | 16 November | First electric tramway in Liverpool opened |
| 1899 | 3 August | First electric tramway in St Helens opened |
| 1900 | 27 May | First electric tramway in Bootle opened |
| 1900 | 20 June | LOR Crosby tramway opened |
| 1900 | 18 July | Southport Corporation starts electric tramway operation |
| 1900 | 19 July | Liverpoool Pier Head tramway loops in operation |
| 1901 | 4 February | Birkenhead Corporation electric tramways opened |
| 1901 | 1 April | Wallasey tramways municipalised |
| 1902 | 17 March | First electric tramways in Wallasey opened |
| 1902 | 27 August | Last Liverpool horse bus withdrawn |
| 1902 | 6 December | Last Liverpool horse trams withdrawn |
| 1903 | 3 May | Electric operation started on Mersey Railway |
| 1903 | 18 May | Through tram service Liverpool-St Helens started |
| 1904 | 22 March | Electric services started on L&YR Liverpool-Southport line |
| 1905 | 2 July | LOR extended to Seaforth & Litherland L&YR |
| 1905 | 11 December | First Mersey Railway motor bus service started |
| 1906 | 2 February | LOR/L&YR Dingle-Southport through service started |
| 1906 | 3 December | L&YR electric trains extended to Aintree via Kirkdale |
| 1907 | February | L&YR started motor bus service Blundellsands-Crosby-Thornton |
| 1907 | 8 July | Mersey Railway motor bus services ended |
| 1909 | 1 October | LYR electric service extended to Maghull |
| 1911 | 1 January | Liverpool Corporation acquires Woolton Motor Omnibus Company |
| 1911 | 3 July | LYR electric service extended to Town Green |
| 1913 | 12 July | LYR electric service extended to Ormskirk |
| 1914 | 27 September | First 'grass tracks' on Liverpool tramways opened |
| 1919 | 6 June | Ribble Motor Services registered |
| 1919 | 12 July | First Birkenhead Corporation motor bus service started |
| 1919 | 1 October | St Helens Corporation takes over tramways |
| 1920 | 3 April | First Wallasey Corporation motor bus service stated |
| 1921 | 19 March | First joint Wallasey-Birkenhead bus service started |
| 1923 | 17 August | First St Helens Corporation bus service started |
| 1923 | August | Waterloo & Crosby Motor Services start operations |
| 1925 | 31 December | Last cars on LOR tramway |
| 1927 | 11 July | First St Helens Corporation trolleybuses started |
| 1928 | 17 October | Liverpool Corporation Edge Lane works opened |
| 1929 | 13 March | Merseyside Touring Company started Liverpool-Bootle bus service |
| 1930 | 8 June | Merseyside Touring Company purchased by Ribble |
| 1930 | 31 December | Waterloo & Crosby Motor Services wound up |
| 1931 | June | Agreement between Liverpool Corporation and Ribble |

| 1931 | 30 September | Merseyside Touring Company ceases bus operation in Liverpool |
|------|--------------|---|
| 1933 | 1 July | Liverpool municipal airport at Speke opened |
| 1933 | 30 November | Last Wallasey Corporation trams withdrawn |
| 1934 | 18 July | Mersey Tunnel opened |
| 1934 | 31 December | Last Southport Corporation trams withdrawn |
| 1936 | 31 March | Last St Helens Corporation trams withdrawn |
| 1937 | 17 July | Last Birkenhead Corporation trams withdrawn |
| 1938 | 14 March | Electric operation started on Wirral lines |
| 1938 | 20 August | Liverpool-Egremont ferry service withdrawn |
| 1945 | 7 May | Birkenhead Town station closed |
| 1948 | 31 May | Passenger service ended on Alexandra Dock branch |
| 1951 | 15 February | Last trams in Bootle withdrawn |
| 1952 | 7 January | Passenger service ended on Aintree-Southport line |
| 1956 | 13 May | Night bus service started through Mersey Tunnel |
| 1956 | 30 December | Liverpool Overhead Railway closed |
| 1957 | 14 September | Last Liverpool Corporation tram services withdrawn |
| 1958 | 1 July | Last trolleybuses in St Helens withdrawn |
| 1960 | 4 January | Seacombe branch closed |
| 1962 | 18 June | Electric services inaugurated Liverpool Lime Street-Crewe |
| 1964 | | Last regular commercial traffic carried on Leeds & Liverpool Canal, Liverpool and Wigan |
| 1967 | 6 November | Birkenhead Woodside station closed |
| 1969 | 1 April | Merseyside Passenger Transport Authority set up |
| 1969 | 1 November | Merseyside Passenger Transport Executive set up |
| 1969 | 1 December | Municipal transport undertakings of Liverpool, Birkenhead and Wallasey vested in Merseyside PTE |
| 1971 | 28 February | Liverpool Riverside station closed |
| 1972 | 30 January | Agreement reached for transfer of Crosville and Ribble local services to Merseyside PTE |
| 1972 | 15 April | Last train services to Liverpool Central withdrawn |
| 1974 | 1 April | Southport and St Helens incorporated into Merseyside PTE |
| 1977 | 30 April | Liverpool Exchange station closed |
| 1977 | 2 May | Liverpool Moorfields station opened; electric services started to Kirkby |
| 1977 | 9 May | Merseyrail 'Loop' opened |
| 1978 | 3 January | Electric rail services started to Garston |

142

# Index

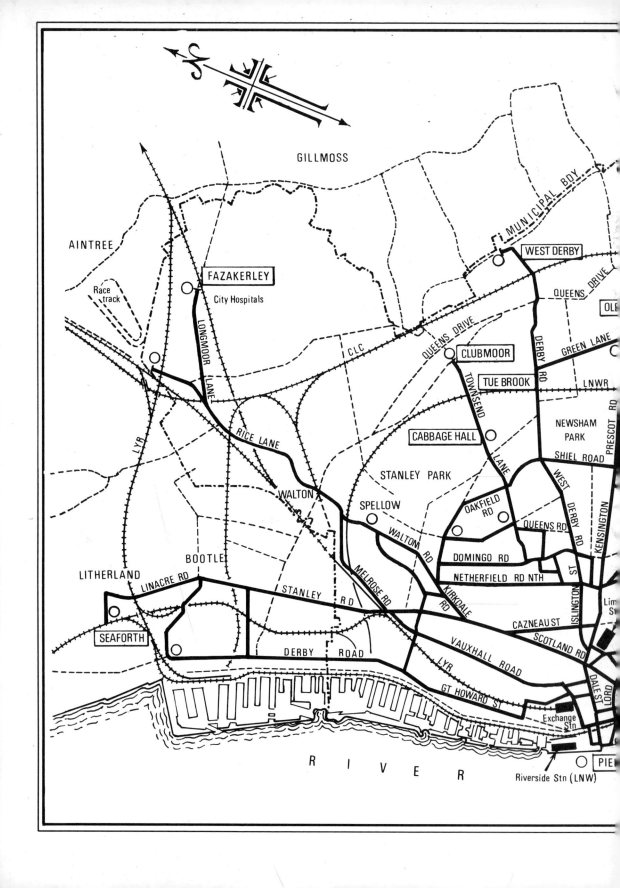